Making & Selling

HERBAL
CRAFTS

Making & Selling
HERBAL
CRAFTS

Tips · Techniques · Projects

Alyce Nadeau

Sterling Publishing Co., Inc.   New York
A STERLING/LARK BOOK

*This book is dedicated to the memory of my darling Louie:
my soul-mate, master teacher, and beloved husband.*

Editor: Chris Rich
Art Director/Production: Elaine Thompson
Photography: Evan Bracken
Illustrations: Kay Stafford and Alexander James

Library of Congress Cataloging-in-Publication Data
Nadeau, Alyce.
    Making & selling herbal crafts : tips, techniques, projects / by
Alyce Nadeau.
        p.   cm.
    "A Sterling/Lark book."
    Includes index.
    ISBN 0-8069-3174-4
    1. Nature craft.   2. Herbs--Utilization.   3. Cookery (Herbs)
4. Handicraft--Marketing.   I. Title
TT157.N22   1995
745.5--dc20   95-12428
                                                       CIP'

10 9 8 7 6 5 4 3 2 1

A Sterling/Lark Book

Published in 1995 by Sterling Publishing Company, Inc.
    387 Park Avenue South, New York, N.Y. 10016

Produced by Altamont Press, Inc.
    50 College Street, Asheville, NC 28801

© 1995 by Alyce Nadeau

Distributed in Canada by Sterling Publishing
    c/o Canadian Manda Group, One Atlantic Avenue, Suite 105,
    Toronto, Ontario, Canada M6K 3E7

Distributed in Great Britain and Europe by Cassell PLC,
    Wellington House, 125 Strand, London, England WC2R 0BB

Distributed in Australia by Capricorn Link (Australia) Pty Ltd.,
    P.O. Box 6651, Baulkham Hills, Business Centre, NSW, Australia 2153

Contents

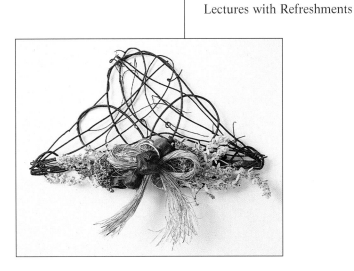

In the Beginning

You don't need to know much about herbs to enjoy this book or to create and sell your first herbal products. When I first became interested in herbs, about ten years ago, I couldn't tell parsley from basil. In fact, my biggest assets were determination and energy. If you can arrange flowers and combine colors and textures, if you enjoy working with your hands, and if you don't mind standing on an herb-strewn floor, then you're already ahead of the game.

I started in this business when funds for my university position were terminated and I couldn't find other employment. One day, my husband, Louie, discovered me standing on tiptoe atop a wooden ladder, painting the eaves of our outbuilding. Although Louie was horrified to think that I might have fallen, I was unconcerned. I'd already read every book in the house and cleaned every household item we owned. To feel useful, I just had to stay busy.

"You need a little vacation," Louie said. After the short one that we subsequently took, I had a dream in which I was making wreaths and working with herbs—very vivid stuff. The dream stayed with me. The next day, I went outside, pulled a vine off the hedge, and wove it into a wreath base. Then I bought silk flowers and greenery at the mall, wired them onto the base, added a bow, and hung the completed wreath on our front door. Naturally my family complimented my efforts. The surprising thing was that friends who visited asked me to make them wreaths, too. Looking back, I marvel at the affection manifested by those requests; my first wreath-making efforts were primitive indeed!

That year, Louie and I spent our annual vacation touring herb shops and gardens. I'd written to tourist bureaus in many states to inquire about herb businesses and fine craft shows. My reward was so much return mail that we were challenged to schedule all the visits we wanted to make.

We started our journey in Michigan, continued through Canada, and then drove down through New England before returning home. On our tour, we saw and smelled enough to hook us indefinitely on herbs and spices. My memories of that trip are of colors, gardens, helpful people, herbal wreaths, and the intense feeling of "I can do that!" When we got back, I proceeded to try.

Through the yellow pages, I found a man to plow up sections of my front and back yards. The agent at the agricultural extension service shared information with me about how to plan my use of these areas and directed me to a class in landscaping. I soaked up information in class, bought gloves and tools, and began digging. I loved it.

On one of those early, beginning days, my sweet next-door neighbor asked if I could "do" a wedding. Smiling all the while, I quickly replied that I could. As soon as she left, I phoned a florist friend to plead for help. He talked me through my first small wedding (silk again), and I was on my way.

The following summer, Louie returned from a business trip with two herb books. I kept these in the bathroom "library," where I read one paragraph at a time. I really wanted an herb garden and spent considerable time studying which plants needed sun or shade, which would dry nicely, and which would return each year. I also discovered a mail-order supplier of dried herbs and everlastings and created my first real herb wreath.

That summer, I bought my first packets of herb seeds at the garden center and planted alternating purple basil and borage around the perimeter of my vegetable garden. Wow! Although I didn't know what to do with the herbs, I was rewarded with visits from bees, butterflies, and hummingbirds that the family watched as we ate our meals on the screened back porch. We also built two trellises and planted our first climbing roses.

Later that year, I participated in my first craft show. Sales were few, but I did receive orders for floral arrangements and wreaths in specific colors. This was the point at which I decided to open a small business in my home. Warm weather found me building my first raised-bed herb garden, in a British flag design, with stone paths and a sundial in the center.

A new friend, Ken, joined me and Louie when we went *wildcrafting* (searching for herbs in the wild). Ken would even return from his business trips with herbs for me to hang and dry. On one occasion, he came back with a small nylon suitcase stuffed full of gray plant material that he'd cut for me in another state. When he complained that

Crafting with herbs is one of life's most satisfying experiences. First, it's a hobby with aesthetic appeal. Second, it's physically gratifying; proximity to fragrance is a sensual pleasure! Last but not least, making and selling herbal crafts can be a fine way to supplement your income.

other passengers on the plane home had switched seats to avoid him, I broke into laughter. Ken's sense of smell had long since been destroyed by repeated exposure to jet fuel; the herbal treasure that he'd brought me was truly foul smelling and had to be carted away to the woods immediately. The odor was somewhat reminiscent of dirty tennis shoes and closed locker rooms!

Ken, like Louie, exists now only in another state of matter, but what a good time we three had in the heat of eastern North Carolina, foraging for herbs and wildflowers.

Before long, I started to receive questions about raised-bed gardening and herbs. My herb library was increasing in size, I began to give lectures at garden clubs, and I joined the fledgling North Carolina Herb Association.

As we started to plan for Louie's retirement, we made short vacation trips into the mountains, seeking an appropriate site for an herb business. When we liked a spot, I would present a real estate agent with my list of seven requirements: proximity to a highway for easy accessibility; open sunny areas that could become gardens; outbuildings for conversion into a studio and shop; zoning for small business, with permission to advertise along the highway; a nice view (without rusted, vine-covered trucks or other eyesores); a downstairs bedroom; water either on or adjacent to the property; and an affordable price.

Within two years, this property had become available, we had placed our other home on the market, Louie had retired, our youngest child had departed for college, and we had embarked on a new lifestyle. My dreams were becoming reality.

Now I do juried craft shows; set up at the farmers' market one morning each week, six months a year; orchestrate herbal weddings; give workshops and lecture-demonstrations; sell wholesale to gift shops; create designs and instructions for craft books; and grow my own herbs.

Making & Selling Herbal Crafts isn't a gardening manual or a textbook on running your own business. In fact, you'll need to visit your public library, an attorney, and an accountant to help you through these very important aspects of making and marketing herbal products. What you will find in this book, however, are

🌿 Herb-garden designs for crafters who want to grow their own materials (and tips on locating suppliers for those who don't).

🌿 Instructions for drying and preserving fresh herbs.

🌿 Guidelines for setting up an efficient workshop.

🌿 Suggestions for packaging your herbal wares attractively.

🌿 Hints on how to advertise your business effectively.

🌿 Extensive information on a wide range of markets for your goods, from craft shows to herbal weddings.

🌿 Instructions for making over 50 herbal projects.

For encouragement, information, and instructions, read on!

From the Ground Up:
Starting an Herbal Craft Business

Herb Gardens

Although you certainly don't need to grow your own herbs (suppliers of dried herbs abound), designing, planting, tending, and harvesting the materials for your herbal crafts can be incredibly satisfying. Public libraries and bookstores are filled with information on gardening, so rather than offer you herb-gardening lessons, I'd like to present you with several possible garden designs and a bit of information on how these designs evolved.

My gardens here in the mountains were started the very day that some herb plants from my former gardens arrived in the moving vans. While I directed the unloading and placement of furniture, my daughter was on her knees near the front entrance, digging holes to receive those plants. It was a start.

For the rest of that month, my husband and I removed fences and tried to bring order to the chaos of neglected land. A dear herb-and-gardening friend visited for a week and helped me to make plans, prune trees, and saw down head-high weeds so that I could hire someone to come in with a mowing machine and reduce the wild grass to manageable levels. We actually crawled on our hands and knees as we fought with those weeds!

With the advent of warmer weather, I started my first formal herb bed, which was roughly triangular in shape, with a sundial in its center. A brick walkway surrounded the sundial and radiated out towards all three sides. Sound easy to create? Well, much like some of the mountains described in my childhood geology books, this garden was built upon rock. It took many more hours than I'd thought possible to remove that rock and prepare the soil.

Then Louie decided that the bricks in the walkway just had to be level. We worked for days on end to accomplish this feat. The result, however, was a fragrance garden, visible from my kitchen windows. During warm weather, especially when raindrops bruised the herb leaves, pleasant aromas floated through the open windows and into the house.

Garden designs depend on many factors: the space, time, and energy you have available, your experience and interest levels, the lay of your land and the amount of sunshine it gets, and the requirements of your selected plants—to name just a few. Some of the everlastings and herbs that I harvest for decorative purposes are simply grown in rows. Others are located in my quilt, fragrance, butterfly-and-hummingbird, silver-gray night, and water gardens. Because I tend to want "one of everything," however, I'll often destroy a well-planned garden area just to give space to a new and untried plant!

When you're ready to start planting, consider your personal comfort. I can remember my wonderful grandmother hoeing her garden while she was wearing a short-sleeved voile dress with a lace collar and cuffs, earrings, high-heeled shoes, and hose rolled just over the knees. As a child, I once asked her why she went to so much trouble when the grocery store was just across the street. Her reply? "Someday you'll understand."

I now do, but rest assured that I don't disguise myself as a lady when I garden. I wear my oldest baggy pants, and I work on my knees. My pants and oversized barn jacket have roomy pockets to hold gardening gloves, twine, shears, markers, tissues, a piece of chocolate, and sometimes even the cordless phone. I wear rubber shoes and cotton or wool socks, and I finish off my outfit with a hat to shade my eyes and keep my hair under control.

Such satisfaction! I'm luckier than most, of course. When I straighten up to wipe the sweat from my eyes

and rest my back, I see the exquisite panorama of the Blue Ridge Mountains surrounding me, and I thank God for letting me be me, here, now.

Whatever I plant, I usually set out in groups of three (Father, Son, and Holy Ghost), and I say a little prayer as I firm the roots into the soil. If I'm working with a plant that's completely out of my frame of reference, I locate each of the three samples in different areas in order to test the results of different miniclimates on that particular plant.

In the next few pages, you'll find diagrams of a few beds I've planted here at Goldenrod Mountain Herbs. Although your own garden designs will be determined by the nature of your property and needs, feel free to draw inspiration from the plans illustrated here.

Entrance Garden

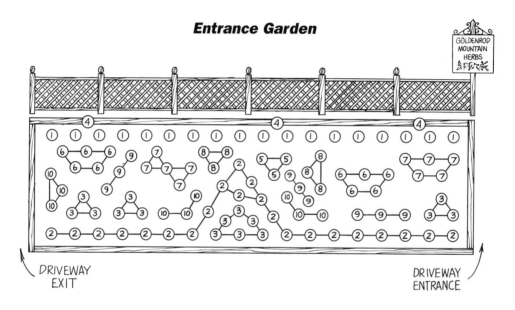

I often give a "show-and-smell" tour to customers who visit my shop and gardens. Starting at my entrance garden (which is bordered by the main road, the driveway entrance and exit, and a white lattice fence), I pick herb leaves and offer them to my guests to crush and smell. I also pass along bits of herb lore and ideas for how to use each herb. By the time we've progressed to my shop, my visitors have collected enough herbs to take home, dry, and blend into a handful of potpourri.

KEY:

1) Goldenrod
2) Silver king artemesia
3) Crested celosia
4) "Old" climbing roses
5) Yarrow
6) Tansy
7) Cleome
8) Oregano
9) Daylily
10) Mints

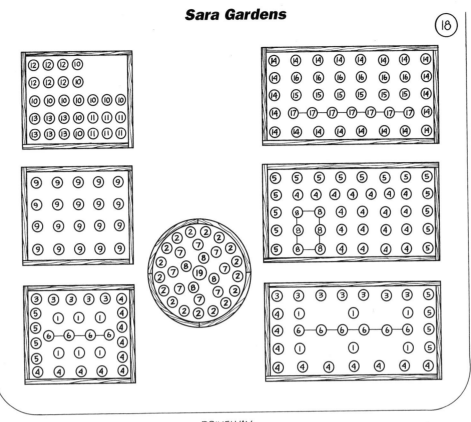

*I*n front of my house are my Sara garden beds, filled with roses, other fragrant flowers, and herbs, and strategically spaced to permit lawn mower access.

KEY:

1) "Old" roses
2) Germander
3) Feverfew
4) Lavender
5) Santolina
6) White yarrow
7) Chives
8) Salvia victoria
9) Sage
10) Anise hyssop
11) Russian sage
12) Pink yarrow
13) Silver king artemesia
14) Thymes
15) Tangerine southernwood
16) Larkspur
17) Ammobium
18) Iris
19) Statue

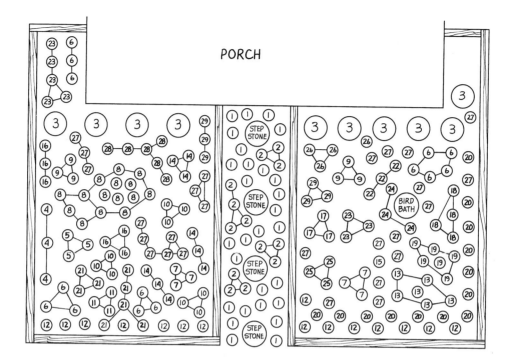

*T*he beds on each side of the stepping stones that lead to my front porch are filled with herbs and flowers of all sorts. One of these flowers, dianthus, was known during the 1300s as gilly flower and was used to make mead. Although they lose their incredible fragrance, I use the hang-dried blossoms in my wedding work. The stepping stones themselves are surrounded by chamomile, which releases its fragrance when it's crushed.

KEY:

1)	Chamomile	16)	Oregano
2)	Ajuga	17)	Yarrow
3)	Arborvitae shrubs	18)	Turtlehead
4)	Lemon balm	19)	Orris iris
5)	Wormwood	20)	Candytuft
6)	Silver king artemesia	21)	Lamb's ear
7)	Shasta daisy	22)	Cleome
8)	Bee balm (monarda)	23)	Mountain mint
9)	Tansy	24)	Sage
10)	Poppy	25)	Blackberry lily
11)	Dianthus	26)	Hollyhock
12)	Nasturtium	27)	Lunaria
13)	Borage	28)	Foxglove
14)	Black peppermint	29)	Columbine
15)	Madonna lily		

Quilt Garden

*P*icture, *if you will, gray stripes separating yellows, pinks, soft greens, purples, lavenders, and reds. In my quilt garden, feathery gray, fragrant silver king artemisia separates rows of colorful, fragrant herbs. Roughly triangular in shape, this garden was designed to be visible from my high bedroom window. Its colors appear as a pleasant blur through the lace curtains, much as if I were looking without my eyeglasses.*

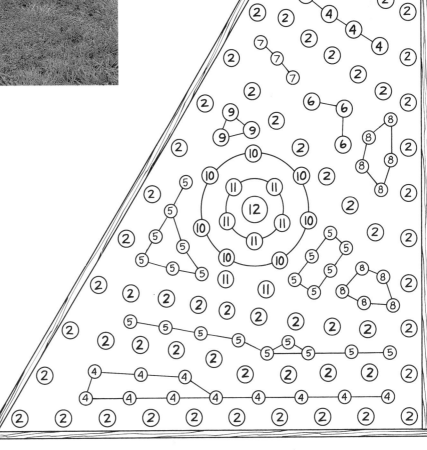

KEY:

1) German sage
2) Silver king artemesia
3) Coreopsis
4) Yarrow
5) Bee balm (monarda)
6) Russian sage
7) Mexican bush sage
8) Dianthus
9) Jewelweed
10) Rue
11) Southernwood
12) Weathervane

Water Garden

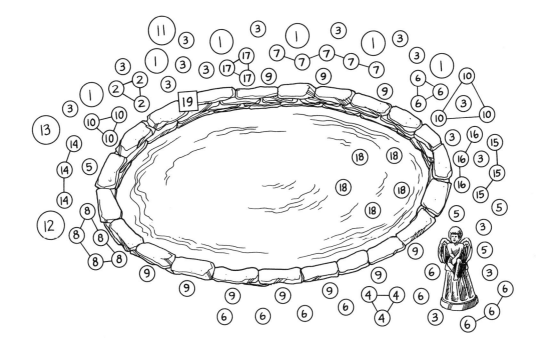

To create this water garden, I first removed enough dirt to fill the back of a pickup truck. Then I sank a free-form, rigid plastic liner into the hole before backfilling the soil around it. An ornamental frog sends forth a pleasant sounding stream of water. Both the pump, which recirculates the water, and the underground electric cord leading to the house are hidden. A backdrop of arborvitae helps focus attention on the water and plants.

KEY:

1) Arborvitae trees
2) Lemon balm
3) Silver king artemesia
4) Lantana
5) Zonal geranium
6) Black peppermint
7) Bee balm (monarda)
8) Borage
9) Pennyroyal
10) Siberian iris
11) Lilac bush
12) Peegee hydrangea
13) Rugosa rose
14) Dutch iris
15) Sweet peas
16) Fern leaf tansy
17) Larkspur
18) Water hyacinth
19) Ornamental frog

Hummingbird/Butterfly Garden

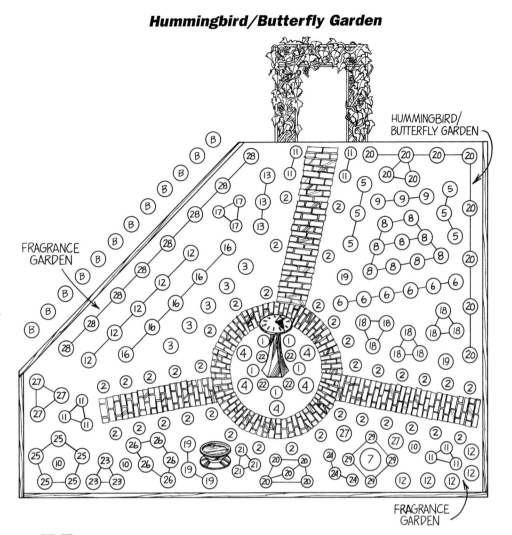

Hummingbird/Butterfly Garden

Fragrance Garden

Fragrance Garden

*H*ummingbirds and butterflies, not to mention bees, are attracted to this lush garden, which I designed in part to lure them into view from the kitchen window. I'm untiringly fascinated by the antics of my tiny visitors. A row of boxwood and a trellis arch separate these beds from ones just below them.

KEY:

B)	Boxwood	11)	Daylily	21)	Mountain mint
1)	Borage	12)	Lemon verbena	22)	Boxwood
2)	Santolina	13)	Hollyhock	23)	Lamb's ear
3)	Lavender	14)	Cosmos	24)	Yarrow
4)	Baby's breath	15)	Dianthus	25)	Powis castle artemesia
5)	Pineapple sage	16)	Lemon grass	26)	Curly peppermint
6)	Lobelia	17)	Tansy	27)	Lemon balm
7)	Comfrey	18)	Delphinium	28)	Thyme
8)	Calendula	19)	Yarrow, Achillea the Pearl	29)	Cosmos
9)	Russian sage	20)	Apple mint		
10)	Butterfly bush				

Silver-Gray Garden

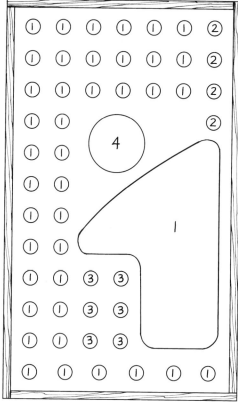

KEY:

1) Powis castle artemesia
2) Tansy
3) Mugwort
4) Garden ornament

*F*or a silver-gray night garden that will reflect as much light as possible, plant gray herbs and white flowers. These may include artemisia; candytuft; daisy; germander; lamb's ear; old-woman wormwood; pearly everlastings; santolina; sages; snow-in-summer; sweet alyssum; thymes (some); and white yarrow. You'll marvel at your ingenuity when you view your work on a moonlit night.

Drying Herbs and Everlastings

In order to preserve freshly harvested plant materials for use in dried arrangements or wreaths, you must remove the moisture from their tissues. Most flowers, herbs, grasses, grains, and berries can be dried fairly easily by hanging, standing, suspending, or spreading them in dry, warm, dark, and airy locations such as well-ventilated attics, large closets, and outbuildings. Cellars and other damp, cool areas will not work, as they can be breeding grounds for molds and mildew. To protect plant colors from fading, keep the plants well away from sunlight as they dry.

Hanging your plant materials is the easiest of drying methods. First, stretch a chain across a room, just below the ceiling. (A heavy-gauge wire will do, but plant materials hooked through a chain link won't slip as they might on a slick wire.)

Next, remove the lowest leaves from a few stems, cut the stems to even lengths, and, using a rubber band, bind the bottom ends together. I lost my first globe amaranth harvest because I tied the stems together with wire instead. As the suspended stems dried, they shrank, and when I

went to check on their progress weeks later, all the plants had committed suicide—fallen from their wires to the floor. I could only use the flower heads for potpourri!

To suspend the bunch for drying, hook one end of a partly unfolded paper clip or a piece of bent wire through the rubber band and slip the other end through a link in the chain.

The length of the drying period will vary, depending on the humidity and temperature, as well as on the amount of moisture in the plant tissues. Check the plants every few days. If they remain in the drying area too long, they may become too brittle for use.

Transfer the dried plants to a cooler location that remains dry and dark. To keep out dust, light, and insects, store your dried materials in loosely covered boxes or in brown paper bags. Be sure to label these containers; you'll be surprised by how quickly they accumulate!

To dry short-stemmed herbs and everlastings, bundle them in a similar fashion and hang them on folding clothes-drying racks. Friends who frequent yard sales watch for racks that I can use for this purpose.

To dry plants the flowers of which are heavier than their stems (Queen Anne's lace, strawflowers, roses, globe amaranth, rudbeckia, and chrysanthemums, for example), use the black plastic plant trays found at greenhouses. Position the trays so that their bottom surfaces are several inches above the floor. Drop the flower stems into the holes in the trays; the flower heads, which won't fit through the holes, will remain in the trays and will dry in an open position.

Hydrangeas and long-stemmed weeds, grasses, and seed pods are best dried in upright containers. Choose a sturdy container with an opening large enough to allow good air circulation around the stems and heads.

Electric dehydrators made for home use are widely available and are especially handy for drying slices of fruits such as apples and oranges.

Silica gel, available from florists and fine craft shops, is a substance used to dry very delicate flowers such as calendula, roses, and zinnias, as it preserves their forms and colors well. Read the directions on the container carefully before you buy.

A mixture of two parts borax and one part dry white sand may be used instead of silica gel. To remove all moisture from this homemade mixture, heat it for two hours in a 200°F (93°C) oven. Then cool and store it for future use.

To preserve leaves of various shrubs, trees, and vines, the glycerine replacement method is often effective. During hot weather, when leaves are fully developed, take 20" to 24" (50.8 to 61.0 cm) cuttings of the branches. Combine two parts hot water with one part glycerine (available at most drug stores). Half fill a wide-mouthed jar with the glycerine-and-water solution. Crush the ends of the cuttings with a hammer and place them upright in the solution. Mark the level of the liquid on the outside of the jar before placing it in a shaded room.

As evaporation occurs and the liquid is absorbed by osmosis, add water to the jar to maintain the original liquid level. As the solution is absorbed into the leaves, they'll become darker, more pliable, and leathery. Before the color change reaches the leaf tips, remove the branches from the solution and spread them out on newspapers to dry.

Absorption times will vary according to the materials used. Thin leaves such as Russian olive and peony may take only two weeks, while thicker leaves such as magnolia may take as long as six weeks. To store the preserved leaves, hang them upside down in a dark location or place them in covered boxes.

Don't bother to try the glycerin method on leaves picked when the weather is cool. Once late-season leaves have started to change color, the life has left them, and they won't absorb the glycerin solution.

My husband Louie used to claim that I could stop my car on a dime if I spotted a wild herb growing along the highway. He wasn't far from wrong. Whenever I travel, I look for useable plants, and, when I find them, I make notes so that I can go back later and gather some for my projects.

You must be alert to discover plants that can be wildcrafted. In my area, goldenrod, pearly everlasting, Joe-pye weed, white yarrow, various mints, wild rose hips, and various pods and grasses are all plentiful.

Wildcrafting

Throughout the world, herbs that grow in the wild (along fencerows, at the sides of roads, in open fields, and in wooded areas) are sought and gathered—a process known as wildcrafting. The famous pioneer Daniel Boone made a living in my mountain area by wildcrafting "sang" (ginseng root), which he sold to traders as a medicinal.

When you search for herbs in the wild, leave yourself time to prepare plants for drying as you gather them. Bunch several stems together, cut the stem ends, and secure the bundle with a tightly twisted rubber band, just as you would with herbs harvested from the garden. Place the bunches in your carrying container, with the bloom ends upright. When you get home, you'll probably be too tired to do anything except hang the bundles up to dry. Fortunately, that's all you'll need to do!

Following are some tips for successful wildcrafting:

❦ Never gather wet materials. To avoid mildew and mold on your dried plants, harvest herbs only on sunny days, after the morning dew has dried.

❦ Dress appropriately. To avoid insect or snake bites, briar scratches, sunburn, heatstroke, and raw hands, wear long pants, a long-sleeved shirt, a hat, gloves, and waterproof boots. If snakes are a danger in your area, make sure those boots are high-tops!

❦ Take along a lightweight container (an open basket, shopping bag, canvas log carrier, or laundry basket), pruning shears or your favorite clippers, rubber bands, cotton gloves, a damp washcloth or premoistened towelettes for cleaning yourself up, insect repellent, sunblock cream, and a thermos filled with drinking water.

❦ Bring along a friend for help and fun.

❦ Seed heads and fluff from blooms will cover everything in your car, so spread out some newspapers over the seats.

❦ Don't pick plants growing in public areas such as state parks and never pick all of anything. Leave enough plants to produce another year's crop for future foraging. Several years ago, a wise American Indian shared with me his belief that the Spirit has placed on the earth a cure for everything that causes harm or illness. Because we haven't discovered all these cures, the Indian insisted that one should forage only one third of a given plant, leaving a third to reproduce and another third for people to study and admire.

Locating Sources for Materials and Supplies

If you don't grow your own herbs, you'll need to find a reliable source for them. You'll also need various items for your workshop and wares—items that you'll find described in other sections of this book. Unfortunately, many suppliers have minimum-order requirements that will place their goods out of your financial reach. Don't be discouraged, though. Continue your search, and you will be rewarded.

One of your best resources for all sorts of materials is a local, state, or international herb group. Join up! By networking at the conventions, you'll get many questions answered, and fellow members will point you down the right paths.

You should also purchase the *Herbal Green Pages: An Herbal Resource Guide*, edited annually by Maureen Rogers. This publication, distributed by the Herb Growing and Marketing Network (address on page 127), is worldwide in scope and contains lists of publishers, associations and societies, periodicals, information services, educational programs, botanical gardens and arboretums, organic information sources, and suppliers of everything from packaging materials to floral and craft supplies. The Network is a membership organization. As a member, you may list your own herb business along with any information about it that you wish dispersed.

Wholesale florists often carry dried herbs and everlastings, wreath bases, decorative accent pieces, ribbons, foliage, baskets, vases, tissue, boxes, fresh flowers, wire, floral tape, and seasonal merchandise. You'll usually find wholesale florists listed in the yellow pages. When you visit them, take along your checkbook, a business card, and the wholesale tax certificate issued by your state. This certificate, by the way, is your license to do business and is provided by the state in which you reside. With a wholesale tax number, you can purchase goods at wholesale prices and resell them in your finished products. When you sell these products, however, you must collect tax money and remit it to the state. Your State Department of Revenue can give you more specific information.

Craft shops and suppliers are also listed in the yellow pages. They generally offer ribbons, scissors, glue guns, wreath bases, fabric, baskets, containers, vases, and more. I visit craft stores periodically just to see what new trends are developing and what colors are in vogue.

For gorgeous ribbons and cords, check at ribbon outlets. You'll need boxes for packaging wreaths, too. To save on money and storage space, order these in wholesale lots. They'll arrive flat and are assembled and taped when you're ready to use them. Some are assembled with tabs and don't even require taping.

Many local libraries keep up-to-date books that list wholesalers around the world. Just ask your friendly librarian for help. Searches elsewhere may require a bit of detective work. When you're in a shop and see an attractive tin that looks ideal for one of your herbal tea blends, for example, turn the tin over, and copy the manufacturer's name from the label. Then get the phone number from information and call the company. Ask right away if they have a toll-free number and call back on it if they do! Ask for their current catalogue and for their minimum-order amount. Then settle back to wait for the post office to deliver the catalogue, and you're almost in business.

Setting Up Your Workshop

Whether you're preparing to make a few special wreaths or several hundred sachets, when you set up your work space, pay attention to the one rule that never seems to change: You can't have enough space. Trust me! Your work will expand to fill whatever is available, so give it as much as you've got. You'll need space to work in, space in which to dry and store your various materials, and space for your finished projects.

When I first started crafting, my work space was a waist-high counter in my husband's shop area in the garage, where open doors and windows provided a pleasant breeze during warm weather. As colder days approached, I sought a heated work area, and, with my family's permission, settled on the dining-room table. (Two of the children were away at school, and the rest of the family was now eating in the kitchen or on the back porch.) I protected my new work surface with blankets and plastic, and Louie built me an easel to hold my wreath bases as I worked on them. I dried and stored herbs in the attic and outbuilding, I displayed my finished products in one section of the large living room, and we used the den to entertain guests!

When we moved to the mountains, I was delighted to have a two-story outbuilding to use as a studio and shop. Louie constructed storage shelves and counters for the upstairs studio, and we enhanced the downstairs shop area by installing shelves, a cupboard, tables, and, for even more display space, lattice screens on the walls.

I still needed space to store packing boxes and garden tools and supplies, but Louie kindly loaned me part of his workshop. My promise to him was to keep the shop and our home separate this time round, but now that I'm alone, I dry herbs upstairs in the house and have my office up there, too.

No matter how you organize the space that you have, bear the following tips in mind:

❧ Your work area must be well lit, but your herb-storage area should be relatively dark. If your work and storage areas are one, focus spot-lighting on your immediate work space, or store your herbs in brown paper bags to protect them from light.

❧ Every object related to your herbal crafts should have a designated space of its own and should be returned to that space when you're through with it.

table or two in my kitchen, bring in my tools, and carry in boxes and bags of herbs. Even when the weather is mild, I'll sometimes set up a card table in front of my easy chair so that I can make pomanders or fill sachet bags while I watch an old movie on the television. You'll also find me in my kitchen when I need to bottle vinegars, mix up potpourri, or make teas and culinary blends. No matter where you work, make sure that there's an electrical outlet nearby. You'll need one for your glue gun and drill.

🌿 Indulge in a cleaning frenzy once in awhile! Sweep, vacuum, dust, and restore order. When I first started in the herb business, I salvaged every tiny scrap of dried material for potpourri or hot-glue work. Now I view this once-cherished material as "stuff," and I relegate it first to the floor, and, after a cleaning frenzy, to the trash bin.

🌿 Provide an area outside your work space where you can view each finished project for a few days before packaging it for sale. Walk around the project, study it from all angles, and decide whether or not it needs improvement. Not until you're completely satisfied should you wrap and label it.

Tools and Equipment

You won't need an elaborate tool collection or much equipment in your workshop. In fact, except for a pick machine (see page 25) and an electric drill, your tools won't differ much from those that any floral crafter keeps on hand. You will need

🌿 Three power tools: either a hot-glue gun or low-melt model; an electric drill with assorted bits; and a radio, for pleasant music! I prefer the low-melt glue gun as it's less likely to cause burns. If you use the high-tempera-ture gun, keep an aloe plant nearby. Slice open a leaf and apply the soothing juice to any burn.

🌿 Hand tools: a sharp knife, a pair of pliers, scissors, wire cutters, and surgical tweezers. The tweezers will help you hold small items as you apply hot glue and posi-tion them on your project. They're also useful for thread-ing yarn in and out of grapevine wreath bases.

🌿 Unless you farm your sewing out, a sewing machine. With it, you'll make fabric covers for products such as Spicy Hot Pads and Mug Mats (pages 62 and 64 to 65).

🌿 A spray bottle. Mist your dried materials with water before you work with them so that they won't crumble.

🌿 Your work area should include at least one waist-high counter or a comparable flat surface. Even a sur-face as small as a lap tray will do if you keep it clear enough to work on. Ideally, the floor should be one that's easy to sweep clean.

🌿 Keep your tools and most frequently used materials within easy reach of your work surface. When I stand at my studio counter, I'm almost completely surround-ed by dried materials, which hang from rafters, peek out of brown paper bags stacked on shelves, and lurk in baskets and buckets nearby. Boxes and racks hold ribbons, and wreath bases are suspended all around.

🌿 Drive a long nail into the edge of your counter and keep a spool of ribbon on it. You'll find that the nail acts as a third hand when you need two to make a bow or wind ribbon around a bouquet handle.

🌿 If your workshop isn't heated, plan on doing at least some of your cold-weather work elsewhere. When ice, snow, and bitter temperatures arrive, I set up a card

A bag holder. Designed to help you reduce clutter, this item sells well, too! It's actually a 5" by 15" (12.7 by 38.1 cm) cloth tube with a handle and is used to store empty plastic bags. Its top border consists of a hollow core made with patterned ribbon and filled with fragrant herbs and spices. The lower end of the tube is elasticized so that you can pull the bags out one at a time.

A trash container. Don't let flammable bits of dried plant materials accumulate; empty the trash frequently.

If you plan to grow and dry your own herbs, don't forget to add gardening tools and folding racks to this list. Other tools might also prove useful, but I manage well with these basic items.

Materials and Supplies

Before stocking your workshop, browse through the projects in this book and decide which ones you'd like to make and sell. Then make a list of what you need. For my own craft work, I keep the items in the following list on hand:

Dried herbs and spices. Though this may sound neurotic, I recommend keeping your spices sorted in alphabetical order. You'd be surprised by how much time it takes to find what you need when materials aren't organized in this fashion!

Wreath bases, including wire frame bases with clamps (especially useful for making swags); straw bases, which come wrapped in plastic; faux evergreen bases; and birch spiral bases

Floral foam, a gray or green porous material that can be purchased in block form and cut with a knife to fit a basket or floral container. Stems inserted into the foam will stay where they are without wobbling. Oasis foam, a version that holds many times its own weight in water, is used with fresh flowers. Sahara foam is designed for use with dried materials.

Floral picks, pins, tape, and wire. Picks, which look like long toothpicks with a length of wire attached to one end, will come in handy if you don't own a pick machine. Pins are U-shaped and hold dried materials against a straw or foam wreath base by wedging them tightly against the surface. Floral tape, available in light or dark green, brown, and white, is for binding stems to one another and for wrapping materials onto a wire wreath base. Also purchase 20-gauge spool wire and floral wire in assorted lengths and gauges.

Sewing supplies: Thread and fabric for products with fabric exteriors. I'm not a seamstress, so I have my sewing done elsewhere.

Display materials: Spray fixatives, available at wholesale florists and craft shops, for protecting finished wreaths and floral arrangements from moisture and dust; tins or other covered bins for keeping bulk potpourri and tea blends safe from light and dust. (I use these as mixing containers, too. Note that herbs or flowers must be bone dry before they're mixed and placed in closed containers.)

For decorative work: Birds (the artificial kind!) and bird cages to use as accents on wreaths; candles to be sold with herbal candle rings; glass balls to decorate as Christmas ornaments; hats to be decorated for bridesmaids or sold as decorative items for the home; ribbons in different widths, colors, and styles, including white satin ribbon for weddings and fancy French wired ribbon (a malleable ribbon with wire sewn into its edges) for gift packaging; spray paint for coloring baskets and hats; tulle, available in rolls 6" (15.2 cm) wide and 50 yards (45.7 m) long from wholesale florists. (I wrap straw wreath bases in tulle to prevent them from shedding.)

Wedding supplies, including satin leaves, lace cuff ruffles, plastic-handled bouquet holders, ropes for garlands, pew clips, and plastic wreath hangers for use on doors

Miscellaneous project supplies: Bottle caps, a hand-held capper, and corks, all necessary for bottling herbal vinegars; chenille stems (also known as pipe cleaners) for making wreath hangers and for attaching materials to wreaths; hot glue, which comes in stick form, for your glue gun; fragrance oils, for adding fragrance to dried materials. (I keep my oils in a large, open basket so that they're easy to move from place to place); vases for wedding florals and custom arrangements for homes and businesses; yarn for attaching materials to grapevine and twig wreath bases.

I'm also careful to keep a supply of packaging and office materials, and I have an entirely portable, home-made display booth that I take to farmers' markets and craft fairs. You'll find these items described in up-coming sections.

Wiring picks in place by hand is fine for hobbyists, but it's just not cost-effective when you're making dozens of projects at one time. Although a manually operated pick machine, available from wholesale florists, isn't inexpensive, it's easy to use and will cut your project assembly time in half. Special toothed metal picks known as "brads" are first loaded into the machine. Then a stem is positioned over the brad, and the machine wraps the teeth of the brad around it.

Successful Packaging

No matter where you sell your herbal crafts—in your own shop, in someone else's, or at an outdoor fair or herb fest—packaging them attractively is tremendously important. To catch the attention of potential customers, packaging must be neat, pretty, well labeled, colorful, and original in design. In addition, packaging may need to protect your products from dust or daylight or both. What will you need in order to meet these requirements?

❧ Plastic bags, zip-type or plain, are best for products (such as loose potpourri) that can't be wrapped in cellophane. Showcase wreaths and cakes in really large plastic bags.

❧ Cardboard boxes are useful for storage and mailing. If you sell homemade cakes, you'll also want custom boxes for mailing them. Although I display wreaths without any wrapping, once a customer has purchased one, I place it in a cardboard box and cover it with tissue. When the wreath must be shipped, I wire it right into the box so that it won't shift in transit.

❧ Transparent plastic boxes and glass or plastic jars of various sizes, stenciled brown-paper bags, and fancy, imprinted plastic bags all serve to keep your wares clean but visible. For culinary blends, I purchase small glass or plastic bottles that come with shaker tops and twist-on lids. When you're just starting out, do what you can based on your cash-flow situation. Later, do whatever proves successful!

❧ Baskets. To prepare gift baskets, I first package the individual culinary or personal beauty items and then wrap each one in cellophane, tying it closed with fancy wired French ribbon. Then I place a layer of *excelsior* (or wood shavings) in the bottom of the basket and arrange the items on top. Recipes to help customers get started with new products go in next. Finally, the entire basket is wrapped in cellophane and decorated with an embellished bow.

❧ Tins and opaque jars for protecting herbal teas and culinary blends from light. Alternatively, place teas in small plastic bags, and tuck the bags into mugs or teapots.

❧ Vinegar bottles. The Department of Agriculture and the Food and Drug Administration insist on the use of new, sterilized bottles for vinegars. I purchase imported ones from Europe.

Because exposure to sunlight breaks down the molecular structure of herbs in vinegars, my labels contain a cautionary statement to this effect. (Young brides, especially, are prone to leave herbal vinegars in windows and treat them like stained glass.) Along with every bottle, I also include a recipe that calls for vinegar, a touch that my customers appreciate.

Vinegar bottles may be capped or corked. When possible, I cap the bottles and attach fresh corks separately by wrapping them in squares of tulle and tying them to the bottle necks. Capped bottles tend to travel more safely than corked ones!

❧ Foil paper, tissue paper, and clear cellophane. Foil works well for fancy gift wrap; tissue makes an attractive and protective liner for products packaged in boxes; and clear cellophane protects products from dust but leaves your wares visible to the customer.

❧ Decorative embellishments. At the very least, I tie each wrapped package with a bow. On many products, I tuck silk ivy leaves and a small spray of silk flowers into the bow and add a string of pearls.

🌿 Tags and labels. Every piece of my work comes with either a hanging tag, attached with a golden, elastic cord, or a gummed label. Both list the product name, price, and, when appropriate, ingredients. If special care or use instructions would help the customer, I include them, too, on a "customer instruction card" (see page 53), and I often include recipes with culinary blends. At the farmers' market, I place cards with similar information next to items such as gift packages.

When customers request special gift packaging, I'm happy to oblige. I line the gift box with tissue paper, place the gift inside, and cover the box with a floral-design wrapping paper. A pretty wired bow goes on top, and into it I tuck a small herbal nosegay with its stem ends wrapped in floral tape—not quite a corsage, but almost! Both customers and recipients are happy with the results, and I never get complaints about my gift-wrap charges. (I always let the customer know in advance what my fee will be, of course.)

Advertising

Packaging is only one form of advertising. As you try out the others, remember that building a good reputation is a continual process, one in which your attitude is all-important. Be pleasant with your customers, accept small defeats gracefully, learn from your mistakes, and always maintain high-quality merchandise.

I am not an advertising expert and have taken no formal business courses; I've learned a great deal, however, from experience. Because I'm basically a one-person show (sometimes two, sometimes three—sewing and gardening can get ahead of me), I keep my paid advertising to a minimum. People come to know of me by word of mouth, through the yellow pages, from seeing my name appear in books that carry my designs, and from seeing my logo.

Satisfied customers tell others about my work and make appointments to bring new people to see my gardens and shop, which are open as long as the weather isn't freezing cold. Time permitting, I serve my visitors cups of tea and invite them to sit in my kitchen and watch the birds through the tall windows. Tourists return annually to see what's new and to say hello. As the years pass, friends bring their children to meet me, and herb-loving friends from organizations to which I belong stop by when they vacation in the mountains. I recently entertained my first bus tour, too!

The yellow pages advertise my presence to people passing through the area. I also receive calls (I'm amused by the number) from people who wildcraft medicinal herbs and who would like to sell them to me. I never buy—or sell—medicinals, but at least these people know that I'm around. I assume they'll get in touch when they need high-quality herbal crafts!

Several of my herbal designs have been published in craft books. As a result, I receive letters and phone calls from gift shops and individuals throughout the country. Some readers want to place orders; others request information or jobs. I try to respond to all inquiries and to encourage people to get involved with herbs.

Perhaps my most effective advertising tool is one used by all professionals—a business logo. Designs for logos are available from advertising agencies, printers, and public-library books. Select a logo that reflects who you are and what you plan to emphasize in your business, and pay close attention to design details. Also, to emphasize the logo itself, leave some unfilled space around it.

Once you've selected a logo, have it printed on your business cards, on your stationery, and, most importantly, on the tags and labels that will go on every piece of your work. Check with several printers; you'll find a vast range of prices and will naturally want to take advantage of the best deal you can find. In time, people will automatically associate your logo with you and your work.

I also record names and addresses from checks I've received. Although I haven't used this ongoing mailing list yet, I plan to notify the people on it of the next herb fest I host. When I get a computer, I may also design a catalogue and expand into mail order.

Other advertising techniques are worth considering, though some tend to be quite expensive.

🌿 Monthly newsletters mailed to all your customers

🌿 Advertisements in national magazines

🌿 Contracts for standard ads in newspapers—ads that always run in the same space

🌿 Mailings to customers regarding new products and sales and impending workshops and seminars

🌿 Billboard advertisements

🌿 In-store, after-hours events to which customers are invited with their friends and at which they receive gifts or percentage discounts on store items

🌿 Book-signing parties, where customers get a chance to meet authors

🌿 Phone calls to alert valued customers to your new products

Setting Up an Office

No matter how large or small your business is, you'll need an office area that is private and undisturbed. When you look for something there, you should be able to find it! You'll spend quite a bit of time in this space, so be sure that it's comfortable, too.

Your accountant will need detailed, accurate records from you—records of all the money you've taken in and paid out. Ask for and keep receipts for every purchase you make. Have your accountant help you set up a ledger. He or she will also let you know which expenses are tax deductible.

In addition to keeping financial records for tax purposes, you'll want to record and file the information on every personal check that you receive from customers so that you can attempt to retrieve money due to you if a check bounces. A system for keeping addresses may also prove useful for advertising purposes.

Obviously, a computer will go a long way towards simplifying and shortening the time you spend in your office, but our parents and grandparents lived without them, and so can we. If you can't afford to go high-tech, make yourself a cup of tea, sharpen your pencils, and get down to business.

Legal and Money Matters

Whether you plan to run a retail shop or sell your goods elsewhere, setting up your own business requires time, money, professional services, and caution! Be sure that you have enough money to sustain you for one year without having to count on your business for an income, and consult professionals at every step, including attorneys, accountants, and the personnel at appropriate state and/or federal agencies.

Running a retail shop takes more physical energy than doing shows and markets away from home and also requires greater overhead expenditures and a larger inventory. Your shop must be cleaned and the stock rotated on a regular basis so that returning customers will stay interested in your merchandise. Unless you schedule hours by appointment (as I do), you'll also need to have a clerk on hand to wait on your customers.

If you limit your sales to shows, herb fests, and farmers' markets, you can leave your display screens, tables, and unsold inventory in your van most of the time. Although you'll need to make products between sales events, you'll have more control of your time than you would if you had to tend an open shop.

As a business owner, whether you run a retail shop or not, you must comply with all laws and regulations relating to small businesses. Check first with your attorney and then with the local, state, and federal agencies to which he or she may direct you. Don't be afraid to ask questions or to find out which questions you should be asking!

You'll need to check your zoning, for example, to make sure that a craft business is permitted in the area where you'd like to work. Your county manager can help with this matter and can tell you whether or not you'll be permitted to put up business signs along the highways or roads near your proposed site. He or she will also direct you to the other personnel you must meet and will probably hand you several pages of printed matter related to starting and operating a business. Read everything that you're given, as it's likely to contain important information.

Before you can be licensed to do business, you must name your business and register that name (known as your *assumed name*). Check at the courthouse to see if the name you've selected is already in use; clerks will show you how to make this search. You can be sued if you use a business name that is exactly like—or even almost like—an existing one, and being forced to change your name can prove costly; you'll need new signs, new licenses, new business cards, and more.

To help people find you more easily, try to incorporate your location into your business name. If this isn't feasible, you might want to incorporate your personal name. In any event, take care of naming your business as soon as possible. When you know which name you want, your attorney will register the name at the courthouse and guide you through the other legal aspects of starting your business, such as securing local, state, and federal licenses and obtaining a federal identification number, which is necessary if you plan to hire employees.

Once you have a business name, open a checking account in that name, preferably at a bank other than the one in which you keep your personal account. Bank personnel can and do make mistakes, so it's best to keep your personal and business finances entirely separate.

Find a good accountant to guide you in tax matters, record keeping, financial decision making, budget preparation, inventory control, setting up forms for monthly and quarterly reports, and—if you plan to hire anyone—payroll decisions. Your attorney or banker can probably refer you to several. Choose someone who will empathize with you as a small business owner and who is qualified, able, responsible, experienced, and successful.

Liability insurance is a must. You need protection to cover your merchandise and any accidents on your property or at shows. If you don't have health insurance through other sources, you may wish to purchase it for yourself now.

The costs of doing business are not insignificant. As you begin to understand what they are, you may choose to stay small!

To Market, To Market: Selling Your Herbal Crafts

Your Own Shop

Designing the interior of a retail shop doesn't require a massive budget. My own shop, which is located on the ground floor of a two-story building on my property, provides a good example.

At the entrance is a counter with an area adjacent to it for wrapping and packaging my products. My cash box hides beneath the counter on a shelf.

I've painted the interior walls white, covered the three windows with lace, and softened the overall effect by scattering lace and antique linens here and there.

In addition to four folding tables, I've added a Hoosier cabinet, a drop-leaf dining table, a library table, a square table, assorted shelves, and a bookcase. The shelves, which can be assembled at different heights, add interest to the display. Except for the drop-leaf, all the other tables are covered to the floor with custom tablecloths so that I can use the hidden space underneath for storage. To create a rainbow effect, I've suspended herbs on chains stretched across the ceiling. The fragrances in this room are amazing!

*U*nder the window and beneath the old linen tablecloth is a secondhand buffet that I attempted, unsuccessfully, to refinish. My husband built the tall shelves that now hold large jars of spices and herbs used in potpourri. Doll chairs, made locally, are nailed to the wall to display handmade dolls, some with herbal themes. Woven rag rugs and baskets of dried herbs cover parts of the painted shop floor.

*T*o display wreaths and swags, I've attached a section of painted lattice to the shop wall. A pine ladder, the rungs of which I've covered with pieces of antique lace, makes a wonderful display shelf for teas, bags of herbal culinary blends, and sweet waters. On the table are books in which my designs appear, herbal vinegars, and a handmade basket filled with globe amaranth and salvia.

Farmers' Markets

A local farmers' market is a wonderful place to sell your wares. In my area, the State Department of Agriculture oversees these markets, each of which charges a nominal membership fee and another small set-up fee for each day that you participate. Our county market is open every Saturday of the growing season. For about six months, I can count on getting up in the dark once a week and driving my loaded station wagon into town for about six hours. What sounds like hard work, however, has become great fun now that I'm well organized.

To locate a farmers' market, check your local newspaper for a listing or contact the State Department of Agriculture for the location nearest to you. Visit the market. While you're there, ask to meet the manager and talk to him or her. Gather all the information you need to help you decide whether you want to sell your herbal crafts there. Following are some questions you might want to ask:

❧ Who is permitted to sell at this market? Our market permits entries only from our county and those adjacent to it. Farmers may sell only what they grow.

❧ When is the annual membership meeting, and what happens at it? At our meeting, a list of rules and procedures is presented to each participant, problems and ideas are discussed, dues are collected, and spaces within the market area are assigned to individual vendors.

❧ How are market spaces allocated? Are they assigned permanently or on a week-by-week basis? Are they sheltered? I'm fortunate enough to have a sheltered, permanent space. My merchandise is protected from all but the heaviest of rains, and because I'm always in the same place, local buyers and returning tourists know right where to find me. When I'm busy at another show or otherwise out of commission, I find a friend to take my place, so that my business—Goldenrod Mountain Herbs—always maintains its presence.

While you're visiting the market, find out what fees must be paid, what sorts of goods are sold, and what kinds of people sell them. Also take note of what customers tend to buy.

Baking for the Farmers' Market

Several years ago, during an economic recession when people were admiring my products but not buying them, I tried to figure out a way to "hook" customers. I watched people for weeks to find out what common thread linked them. Finally, it occurred to me that food was the underlying force that prompted their market visits. I had to decide what food I could offer that would entice people to my booth.

Cakes and muffins—baked with herbs, offered in small quantities, packaged attractively, and made with the finest ingredients—were what I hit upon. (Who would have thought that the cake-baking lessons I begged for from my mother when I was a child would someday help me make a living?) You'll find one of my favorite recipes on page 51.

Before you offer baked goods, find out what your local regulations are regarding the sale of foodstuffs prepared at home. You may be required to have your kitchen inspected, for example. If this is the case and if you have indoor pets or uncertified water and sewage systems, baking may not be an option for you. Check with your farmers' market and with the agencies responsible in your locale.

If your market rules permit it, by all means offer free bite-sized samples to your customers. I present mine on an antique cake stand, which I cover with a paper doily. To keep insects away, I cover the samples with plastic wrap.

What To Take to the Market

Although the list that follows may seem long, remember that booth space at the farmers' market can vary from 8' by 10' (2.4 by 3 m) to 12' by 24' (3.7 by 7.3 m). Sometimes it's even possible—and desirable—to buy two spaces. Although you never want your display to appear cluttered, you must have the props necessary to use your area to its best advantage. As well as packaging materials, bring:

🌿 A metal cash box, change, and a receipt book with carbon paper. Purchase a box with compartments so that you can separate paper money from coins. Don't be short on change! If you're not sure how much to bring, just ask an experienced marketer for a ballpark figure and add a bit more for safety's sake. Use the receipt book to keep accurate records of every item you sell, including its sales price. Tuck a few pens into the box, too; they tend to disappear.

🌿 Business cards and project description cards. Make sure your business logo is on these. Next to baskets of displayed items, place a description card, which should include the item's name, price, and when applicable, ingredients. (By printing the necessary information on it, this card can serve as a customer instruction card, too. See page 53 for an example.)

🌿 Your herbal products. Mine include four 2-gallon (8 liter) glass jars with lids, each filled with a different potpourri. I also display books that carry my herbal craft designs.

🌿 Items for personal comfort, such as premoistened towelettes.

🌿 Booth and display materials, including
 Three folding tables, 24" by 48" (60 by 121 cm)
 A card table
 One or two folding chairs with seat cushions
 Tablecloths or covers for all tables
 A folding, lattice display screen (see page 37)
 Two metal C-clamps to attach a wooden bar
   to the opened screen
 A wooden bar, 30" by 2" (76.2 by 5.1 cm) to stabilize
   the screen. I use bungee cords to attach the bar to a
   permanent post in the farmers' market shed.
 A business sign, which should include your logo,
   business name, and hometown. Display your sign
   where it can be seen easily.
 Several wood blocks in assorted sizes. Use these
   to level tables and screens and to elevate
   display baskets.
 Wooden step shelves, painted white to display
   vinegars
 Double white plastic shelves with linens to cover them

🌿 35

For a stunning visual
display of your herbal
work, suspend it on these
lattice units. The easiest
way to do this is to use
opened paper clips or
chenille stems as hang-
ers. Aim for a balance of
colors, sizes, and shapes
as you create your
arrangement.

Building a Display Unit

Vertical display structures serve several purposes. They block other booths from view and direct the customer's attention to your work; they help create a harmonious, unified, and attractive booth; and they provide backgrounds against which your work becomes the focal point.

The display screens shown (and variations such as the three-section screen that I take to the farmers' market) are not only easy to transport and set up but are also easy to make.

Take a good look at the diagrams. As you can see, this display consists of three screens: a large, flat screen that is lashed with bungee cords to two folding screens. All three sections are constructed from lattice pieces (available at your local building-supply store) that are sandwiched between scrap wood frames to make them sturdier. The frames are stapled or nailed to the lattice and are further secured with metal braces in their corners. To make the two folding screens, framed lattice pieces are attached with hinges.

To hold the folding screens apart once they're stand-ing, a scrap-wood brace is stretched across the top of each one and is held in place with pins dropped into holes drilled through the brace and the upper edge of the frame.

When you get to a show, start by setting up the two folding screens and inserting the braces at the top of each one. Use wood blocks inserted under the standing screens to make sure that they're level. Then hoist the flat screen up about 30" (76.2 cm) above ground level and use bungee cords to lash it to the folding screens.

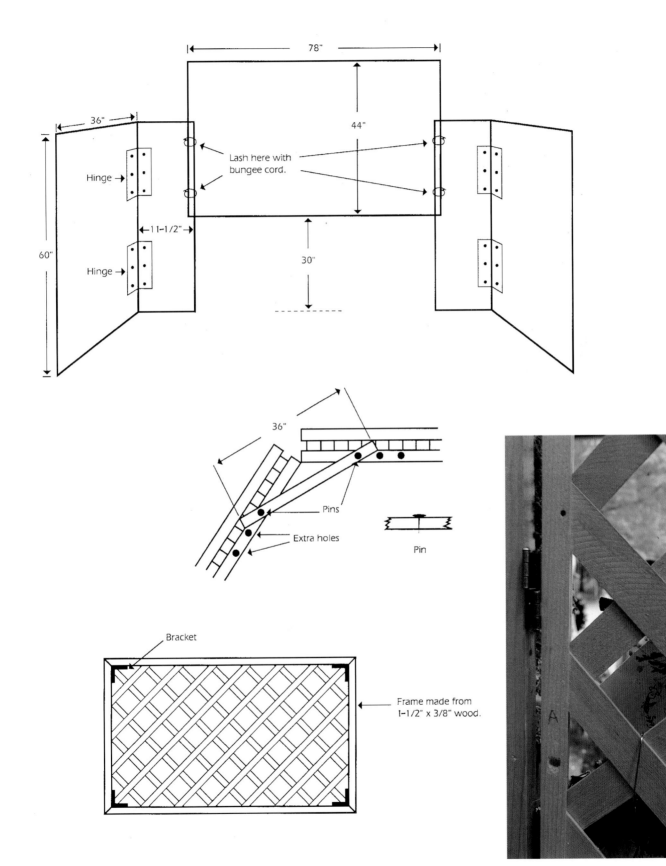

78"

36"

44"

Hinge →

Lash here with
bungee cord.

11-1/2"

60"

Hinge →

30"

36"

Pins

Extra holes

Pin

Bracket

Frame made from
1-1/2" x 3/8" wood.

A

Craft Shows

Juried craft shows and arts-council shows are also excellent places to display and sell your herbal projects. Finding these shows isn't difficult. Look for notices in newspapers and magazines; ask at your local Chamber of Commerce; contact the tourist bureau in your state; ask other craftspeople; and network. If you ask questions, the answers will come back to you.

To be admitted to a juried show, you'll have to fill out an application. This form will present you with a great deal of information, so be sure to read it carefully. If you don't find answers to your questions there, be sure to get them from the people who have organized the show. Find out as much as you can about the following:

🌿 Space regulations. Booth sizes vary widely; some shows offer only one size, while others offer a range of sizes. At some shows, you may be able to buy a double space, but at others, this won't be permitted. Find out whether the cost of the space covers chairs, tables, and electricity as well. In general, corner spaces are the most expensive.

🌿 Time regulations. Find out when set-up and show times are and when you should dismantle your display. There may also be other times during which you should be in attendance. Booth-decoration prizes are sometimes awarded during the hour before the show opens.

🌿 Any decoration methods considered standard for the uniformity of the show. Some shows, for example, may require that all tables be covered in a particular way or may specify maximum heights for framework set up at the sides of the booth.

🌿 Availability of electrical outlets. If you have access to a few, you'll be able to light up your display.

🌿 Whether your display will be guarded overnight. If the show organizers can't guarantee the safety of your wares, plan on having to dismantle your booth each evening so that you can store everything safely in your locked car.

🌿 Liabilities. The majority of craft-show applications contain a paragraph that absolves the sponsors from any responsibility for theft, fire, or accident. If a child burns himself on your hot-glue gun, you'll stand alone when it comes to taking the blame! Ask your insurance agent or accountant for help deciding whether to insure yourself against these types of losses.

🌿 Trash disposal regulations and/or arrangements

🌿 Availability of parking, local lodging, and food and drink during the show

🌿 Whether or not you'll be expected to donate door prizes for drawings held during the day. The sign-up-for-a-free-prize cards provide sponsors with mailing lists for future shows.

🌿 Rules for helpers who may attend the show with you. In an effort to prevent participants from allowing too many of their friends to "help" them in return for free admission, some show sponsors insist that your helpers be designated by name on your application form. They must then pick up name tags when you arrive to set up for the show.

🌿 Tax information. The important thing to keep in mind here is that you must report and pay sales tax on items just as on any other merchandise sold to the public, so keep good records and collect taxes owed to you. Many show applications state that sponsors will not be responsible for collecting state and local sales taxes for merchandise that you sell. Some will have a local tax representative present on the final day of the show who will collect taxes from you. Other sponsors will require you to submit, at the close of each show day, the total sales amount figure for that day.

In most cases, you'll be required to send a show fee with your application. Only after you've submitted your application and fee will your work be accepted for the show; the fee will be refunded only if you're not accepted.

You'll also receive a space assignment. Without exception, craft shows require that your items be handmade; no kits or materials made from kits are allowed. (Unless specifically stated, this rule won't hold true at street fairs or nonjuried craft shows.)

What to Take to a Craft Show

When I participate in craft shows, I bring everything on my farmers' market list, as well as

🌿 An additional folding table, card table, flat lattice screen, and folding lattice screen. I also bring four bungee cords to attach the three screens together, table-cloths to cover all tables to the floor, and extra shelving units now that I have surfaces on which to put them!

🌿 Extension cords, an electrical box with six receptacles, four lights to clip over the top of my booth, several 60- and 100-watt electrical bulbs, and electrical tape to secure cords onto the floor so that people won't trip on them. Existing lighting at indoor craft shows may very well need the boost that these supplies will provide.

🌿 A tool chest, including a staple gun and staples to attach fabric backings to the display screens if backings are required.

Herb Fests

Herb fests are great fun because unlike farmers' markets and many craft shows, they're usually held outdoors under tents. They also tend to attract really interesting people. I have yet to meet a rude or haughty friend of herbs, and any friend of herbs is a friend of mine! The atmosphere is very relaxed. People come to enjoy themselves and to gain information, and they very often have the opportunity to rub shoulders with big-name herbal gurus.

If you're unfamiliar with the area in which the fest will take place, check out the site in advance, and locate a shady spot to request for your set-up. If you don't have your own tent and don't plan to rent one, ask to be placed under a shelter of some kind in order to protect your merchandise from rain and high winds.

Ideally (and this holds true for farmers' markets and craft shows, too), you won't want to be so far away from

the center of activities that people tire or spend all their money before reaching you, or just don't bother to come by at all. Neither do you want to be so close to live music that conversation becomes impossible or so near the kitchen that the smell of food pervades and over-whelms the delightful fragrance of your wares.

At an herb fest, you may be asked to present a short edu-cational lecture or demonstration on an herbal theme to a set number of participants. Accept the challenge! Just be sure to take along adequate supplies to share: herbs to "scratch and sniff," or, if you plan to walk the partici-pants through an herbal project, plenty of materials for every audience member.

When I participate in a craft show or herb fest, I usually wear a pretty jumper over a white blouse with a lace collar. One of the antique petticoats that I collect adds a special touch to my "herb lady" or "mountain lady" costume. If I'm going to be in the sun, I add a straw hat, which I've decorated by wrapping ribbons and herbs round the crown. Sometimes, for a show held indoors, I make myself a little garland of herbs to call attention to my profession. At weddings, once I've completed all the on-site tasks, I change into a "church" dress or suit and add a corsage and earrings.

Take a helper to the fest; you'll definitely want time off to visit every vendor. Ordinarily, you'll find every imaginable herbal item for sale, including plants, pictures, crafts, culinary items, garden enhancements, books and posters, notepaper, bottles and jars, T-shirts, totes, stained glass, pottery, medicinal tinctures, and gathering baskets.

What to Take to an Herb Fest

For herb fests, I add the following to my farmers' market list:

🌿 A tent, unless my space is sheltered. When you rent or buy a tent, first decide what purpose you want it to serve, and then select a tent to match your needs. Shade tents are a bit like umbrellas; they'll protect you from the sun but will offer no shelter from the rain. Other tents are waterproof on top and have optional sides that can be closed in the event of heavy precipitation. Practice setting up your tent in your own backyard so that you'll be familiar with the process and don't forget to include setting-up tools in your tool kit.

🌿 Personal comfort items, including sunscreen, a wide-brimmed hat, sunglasses, a fan, and insect repellent.

A costume isn't necessary in this business, but dressing in a particular way helps people remember you and what you do. Don't be surprised if you find your "look" copied by others, however. Imitation is supposed to be the most sincere form of flattery!

neous supplies out of sight but within easy reach.

🍃 Choose your chair for appearance as well as for comfort.

🍃 Use the back, front, sides, and center of your display units to their fullest potential.

🍃 Examine your projects to determine if they look best from above, below, or at eye level. To create multilevel areas of visual interest and to increase space, arrange wooden boxes or shelves on tables.

🍃 Group items by similar color or use.

Setting up requires an early start. I usually arrive at craft shows, for example, at least three hours in advance, if not the night before.

First I set up the display screens, leveling them when necessary by placing wood blocks underneath them. I arrange my wreaths next, while I'm still able to reach them conveniently.

Next come the card tables and the cloths that cover them. I arrange my products on the tables, grouping them according to their function; potpourris and sachets are placed in one area, and culinary products in another.

Finally, I set up the table where my cash box sits, along with the photo album of my wares. When possible, I like to place a fresh herbal arrangement on this table, too.

Selling Your Wares— and Having Fun

Salesmanship is a skill the basic rules of which aren't all that difficult to learn. Always be open, friendly, and helpful. Take care to appear clean, neat, and well-groomed. Be available to your customers; never read when you're on duty, or they may hesitate to interrupt you with questions and requests for service.

Your sales technique will reflect your personal style. Because I hate high-pressure tactics, I allow people to take their time looking at my creations. If they seem interested, I walk up to them and offer to answer questions or strike up a conversation. I thank my customers for coming by even if they don't purchase anything.

Accept the fact that some people will examine your wares closely, not because they want to buy but because

Setting Up at Markets, Fairs, and Fests

When I first started selling at markets and fairs, I displayed my wares on one folding lattice screen, placed vertically, and on a card table. As time passed, I experimented with other presentation methods and finally arrived at a complete booth design that I could create with a modicum of energy in a minimum amount of time. Finding a design with these qualities was imperative for me because I'm not a natural-born "morning person!"

You'll develop and refine a design that's right for you, of course, but these tips will prove helpful.

🍃 The structures that make up your display (tables, shelves, and free-standing lattice or pegboard units) should be attractive but should focus attention on your herbal crafts, not on themselves. If they're made of wood, make sure they're freshly painted or stained and aren't too heavy to transport.

🍃 Tablecloths should be clean and unwrinkled and should complement the colors of your projects. At shows and fests, cover all tables, ideally with cloths that come down to within 3" (7.6 cm) of the floor, so that you can store your extra inventory and miscella-

they intend to copy your designs. Train yourself to be gracious in response. The more you share, the more you will receive!

Building goodwill pays off later. Offer your card to serious "lookers" and don't be surprised if they contact you later with a special order. When people request custom work, by the way, have them identify their price range for you, and make sure you give them an accurate estimate of what you will charge for the finished product.

No matter where I'm selling my wares, I have an album on hand in which I've mounted color photos of my gardens, some weddings I've done, and a few of my products. Unless I'm displaying my wares in my shop or someone else's, the album sits on a table with my cash box, where it often entices people to stop and chat.

Be professional in keeping your booth swept, neatly arranged, and self-contained. Everything in it, including your chair, should stay within your assigned floor space. When you've sold an item and have run out of replacements, reposition remaining projects to cover the "hole."

If you're required to demonstrate your craft during a show, do so in a manner that is not offensive to others. If you demonstrate wreath-making, for example, don't leave unsightly trash on the floor. Avoid creating safety hazards: flammable piles of herbal debris, electrical extension cords that might cause one to trip, and hot-glue guns that might cause burns if touched.

Set aside some time for networking, either on-site before the sales begin or in the evening at your motel. You'll gather much of value from other participants: information on supply and equipment sources, names and dates of upcoming shows, names of professional organizations and their convention dates, as well as advice and encouragement. At an herb fest, an herbal meal (vegetarian or otherwise, picnic or sit-down) may also be served, and you won't want to miss it!

Let me assure you that this whole endeavor is fun. In fact, the hours I spend at markets, fairs, and fests are almost always some of my most relaxing. Friends stop by the farmers' market to catch me up on their children and grandchildren. Returning customers chat with me, too, and because I arrive so early, I get first pick of the fresh fruits and vegetables for my own kitchen and guests. In many ways, being at one of these sales events is a bit like being at a festival: plenty of color, happy sounds, nice smells, and relaxed customers!

Packing Up and Praying for Fair Weather

I usually begin to dismantle my farmers' market display around noon. (I only stay longer when there's a special festival, such as the summer Firefly Festival, in the farmers' market area.) When I arrive home, I unpack the car before lunch because many visitors come by to see my gardens, and life is easier if I do what needs to be done on a priority basis.

Packing up after a weekend show is a matter of bringing home what didn't sell. Place heavy screens and large wreath boxes beneath lightweight baskets and boxes in your car. After you get home, check your inventory. Keep a list of the products that sell well at each show, so that if you do that show again, you'll know what to bring. Store the leftovers, work to replace stock you've sold, copy your check information for your files, make your bank deposit, and record information for your taxes.

Herbal Weddings

As soon as I'm called about an herbal wedding, I make an appointment for the bride and her mother to come to my house. Before they arrive, I gather photos of weddings I've done, prepare herbal tea and cake, and clear the area of people so that we'll have uninterrupted privacy for our first meeting. I set out a clipboard for taking notes and make sure my price list is on hand.

The purpose of this initial encounter is to gather information. The bride wants to know whether I can make her wedding day memorable for a price she can afford. I want to find out everything that will help me eliminate surprises. Disasters sometimes happen at weddings, and I don't want one to be linked to me! What I do want is for the site to be so lovely and to smell so delightful that

every woman there will want her wedding or her daughter's wedding to be an herbal event.

Besides finding out the dates, times, and locations of the rehearsal dinner, wedding, and reception, I'm interested in getting the following information:

🌿 Names, addresses, and telephone numbers for the bride, the groom, and the party who will receive my bill

🌿 The bride: Color and style of her gown; her preferred floral style (colonial or modern, for example); her preferred style for a headpiece (hat or veil)

🌿 The attendants: How many are expected; the color and style of their gowns; preferred styles for their bouquets; preferred styles for their headpieces (barrettes, crowns, headbands, or combs)

🌿 The flower girl: Color and style of her dress; whether she will carry a basket or bouquet; whether she will wear a flower crown or barrette

🌿 Boutonnieres: Who will require them (groom, best man, ushers, groomsmen, ring bearer, fathers, grandfathers, minister, organist, others); and what their design and color preferences are

🌿 Corsages: Who will require them (bride's mother, groom's mother, grandmothers, wedding director, ladies who serve at the reception, ladies at gift-register and guest-register tables, others); and what their design and color preferences are

🌿 The wedding ceremony: Which decorations, if any, will be provided by other sources, and what they will look like; which areas of the church will require my herbal decorations (main altar, aisles and pews, canopies, candelabrums, aisle runner, windows, foyer, doors, entry doors, kneeling benches, other)

🌿 The reception: Which items the bride would like me to decorate (cake, cake table, cake server, centerpieces, champagne glasses, other)

🌿 The rehearsal dinner: whether the bride would like to have centerpieces or other decorations made

I always insist on getting color samples of gowns before I begin because people can make mistakes in describing color tints and shades—but I can't!

I also ask the bride if she has any special requests. The bride whose wedding is pictured in this book asked me to incorporate the Bible from her mother's wedding into her bouquet. I've also had a bride request the secret addition of a portion of her baby blanket!

Sometimes, photographers take wedding photos of the bride two or more months before the actual wedding date. Make sure you know if an appointment of this type has been set, as the bride will want you to make her bouquet (dried, silk, or fresh) for the photographs.

Many herbs and flowers have acquired meanings over the centuries. By the Victorian era, an entire "language of flowers" had developed, one that enabled lovers to communicate with each other by sending bouquets composed to express particular sentiments—adoration, constancy, and devotion, for example.

The herbal wedding pieces that I create are based on this language, so I give the bride a list of these herbs and

their meanings and let her select the ones she'd like to incorporate into the ceremony. Many books on the language of flowers are available, but the chart on page 47 contains some common examples to pique your interest.

The time of year will influence your choice of flowers, of course; take care not to offer the bride any unrealistic options! During the colder months, you'll probably want to work with a combination of dried herbs and everlastings and fresh flowers secured from your wholesale florist. During the warmer months, you'll use more fresh herbs and flowers from your gardens.

To determine how long your fresh herbs will actually stay fresh, run a test. Early in the morning, gather a few samples of each herb or flower that you'd like to use and place the samples in water. Set the containers in the shade or indoors and watch to see how long it takes the samples to wilt. Leave nothing to chance when you're in charge of wedding decorations!

If the bride agrees, use dried herbs for bouquets, corsages, boutonnieres, herbal wedding wreaths, garlands, and head pieces, so that you can make these items before—not on—the big day. Your life will definitely be easier with the stress of some last-minute projects removed. Having to create everything on site, while contending with photographers and early guests who want to ask you questions and watch you work, might make you wonder if you'd charged enough to compensate for your mental tension!

After my visit with the bride and her mother, I estimate costs and collect a deposit. Do design a payment schedule that is agreeable to your customers and that includes arrangements for complete payment before the bride walks down the aisle. Have your customer sign this contract before you begin work.

As soon as possible after receiving your deposit, visit the church or hall where the ceremony will take place. Take a camera or sketch pad and a tape measure.

🌿 Measure areas where decorations will be needed.

🌿 Check to make sure that carpets and wall coverings won't clash with clothing and proposed flower colors.

🌿 Decide whether to use green or gray as the predominant color in wreaths and swags in order to have them show up against backgrounds when photos are taken.

🌿 Draw diagrams and take photos. Your sketches and snapshots will prove helpful as you construct wedding pieces in your studio.

🌿 Locate the dressing rooms, the area where you'll be creating florals, rest rooms, water sources, and trash containers. Familiarize yourself thoroughly with the area.

Always have a plan of action and follow it as closely as possible. Do as much as you can before the event. Tie bows, for example, to decorate swags, banisters, doors, and tables.

The church may want you to use their altar urns and candelabrums for herbal arrangements, but you probably won't be permitted to remove these from the building. What to do? Create your arrangements in plastic liners and slip the liners into their permanent containers when you arrive at the church. To avoid scratching metal candelabrums, use *chenille stems* (also known as pipe cleaners) to secure greenery and flowers in place.

What to Take to an Herbal Wedding

Be packed and ready to arrive at the church as soon as it's open to you. Bring a "costume" appropriate for the wedding ceremony and all your herbal creations. Also bring:

🌿 Supplies: Chenille stems; extra corsage, boutonniere, and straight pins; floral foam; floral wire; fresh-flower preservative; glue sticks; masking and transparent tape; newspapers

🌿 Tools and equipment: Buckets for transporting water; an extension cord; a garbage can (unless provided); a glue gun; scissors; a sharp knife; wire cutters

Setting Up at a Wedding

When you arrive at the church, unload your car. Cover the floor or carpet in your work area with newspapers. Place the garbage can nearby and spread out your tools and fresh-cut flowers and herbs. Cut floral foam for containers, fill vases with preservative and water, and begin your arrangements. Allow yourself enough time to finish, place all your creations where they belong.

Plan on overseeing the process of pinning on the corsages and boutonnieres and on showing the bride and attendants the best way to hold their bouquets for maximum advantage to viewers. Then, change into a "church" dress or suit, pin on your own corsage, and sit in the back row during the ceremony.

Packing Up

If no photos will be taken after the ceremony (a custom now in vogue), get permission to dismantle the wedding decorations as soon as the ceremony is over and dispense the flowers according to the bride's wishes. After the reception, remove all traces of your presence, and again, follow the wishes of the bride in disposing of the florals. (Large arrangements are often left to be used in the sanctuary on Sunday or are taken to a close relative who was unable to attend the wedding.)

When the wedding and reception areas are clean, load the van, drive home, kick off your shoes, and relax! You've earned a bit of rest.

The *Language* of *Flowers*

ARTEMISIA
Constancy

BABY'S BREATH
Happiness

BAY
Glory

BOXWOOD
Endurance

CHAMOMILE
Patience

COCKSCOMB
Affection

EVERLASTINGS
Never ceasing remembrance

GLOBE AMARANTH
Preference

HYSSOP
Loving sacrifice

IVY
The love of God

LAVENDER
Luck; devotion

LEMON BALM
Comfort

LEMON VERBENA
Herb of Venus; unity

LUNARIA
Money in your pocket

LEMON BALM

ROSES

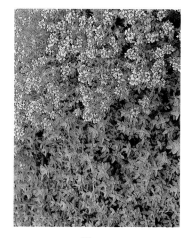

THYME

MARJORAM
Joy

MINT
Eternal refreshment

OREGANO
Substance

PARSLEY
Festivity

PINK
Pure affection

ROSEMARY
Remembrance

ROSE
Love

SAGE
Wisdom; esteem

SALAD BURNET
A merry heart

SAVORY
Interest

SPEARMINT
Warm feelings

TARRAGON
Lasting interest

THYME
Courage

YARROW
Dreams of a loved one

Consignment Sales

Herbal crafters are sometimes invited to place their goods in shops on consignment. The owner of the shop then pays the crafter a percentage of the retail sales price that she or he charges the customers. Usually, the crafter is paid only after an item has actually sold.

As I was taking my first unsteady business steps, being asked for the first time to sell on consignment was a big boost to my ego. When the owner of a florist's shop contacted me, I yielded immediately to her request and worked diligently to supply her with the items she wanted. Imagine my shock when the courts closed her shop doors and seized her inventory the following month. What a lesson!

My advice to you is to check carefully before making any decisions regarding consignment sales. Ask these questions.

🍃 How and when will you be reimbursed?

🍃 What records will be kept and by whom?

🍃 Will you be notified as items are sold so that you can replace them in the shop inventory?

🍃 Will the shop owner tell you when customers request special items?

🍃 Will she tell you when customers express color preferences or make other suggestions that might help you improve your sales?

🍃 When customers want items gift-wrapped, who will provide—and pay for—the necessary materials?

🍃 Is the shop clean and well organized?

🍃 Can you count on the shopkeeper to keep your items clean and fresh, or will they have to be "reworked" after a couple of weeks because they look shopworn?

Only if you are completely satisfied by the answers you get should you consider this sales method.

Sales to Shops

A better way to begin placing your herbal crafts in shops may be to sell them directly to the shop owners. To gather information about possible stores, spend a day visiting them. Dress appropriately, carry a notebook, and record answers to these questions.

🍃 What colors are emphasized in the shop's decor?

🍃 What colors stand out in the shop's inventory?

🍃 Will your herbal items enhance the goods already displayed?

🍃 Are the shopkeeper and employees friendly and helpful with their potential customers?

🍃 Does the atmosphere feel right to you? Does it make you want to stay longer to look around?

🍃 Is the shop clean and well lit?

Make notes as soon as you return to your car so that you won't forget your impressions. After you get home, compare and contrast the shops you've visited and determine which shopkeepers to approach.

Next, package a few of your craft items as attractively as possible. Select two wreaths and four or five other items and take them to the shop you've chosen. Make sure that you're dressed appropriately.

Ask to speak with the manager. When you meet her, introduce yourself, presenting your business card as you do, and ask her if she would like to see your craft items. If you're feeling shy or vulnerable at this point, remind yourself that she can only answer "yes," "no," or "maybe."

If the answer is negative, thank her for her time. There's no point to being pushy; she has your card and may have second thoughts later. If the answer is positive, ask her whether it would be more convenient for her to go out to your car or for you to bring your items into the shop.

Try not to appear too eager as you display your wares, but do provide a list of wholesale and suggested retail prices for them. Assure the shopkeeper that you will sell to no other shop in the immediate area if she will agree to carry your herbal crafts.

Setting Wholesale and Retail Prices

Never sell your work short, but don't put such a high price on your items that the shopkeeper cannot move them. If it's her habit to *keystone* (mark each item up 100%), she's not likely to accept items that are already expensive. Remember that she's paying overhead costs, so don't charge her as much as you'd charge an individual customer. Do set a first-time minimum order, however, and a somewhat lower minimum for subsequent orders.

Pricing products made with homegrown materials is difficult indeed. Out-of-town customers from large urban areas may tell you that your prices are too low. Other customers may tell you that your work is lovely but much too expensive. Listen to these comments, but never change prices on the spot, except perhaps to give an acquaintance your 10% "family" discount or to deduct 10% from sales over a certain amount. Once in awhile, if an item is easy to make, if I have an abundance of left-over materials, and if I'm about to harvest new herbs, I'll run a "special" to reduce my inventory.

You must incorporate into your prices the time you spend growing and harvesting your herbs, but don't be greedy. As you make your calculations, remember psychic income: the pleasure and personal satisfaction accrued from a job well done!

I arrive at my prices by using the formula below, which usually assures me at least a minimum-wage payment for my time.

(Cost of wreath base   Wholesale
 + cost of wholesale herbs   x 2-1/2 =   price of
 + cost of all other materials)   finished wreath

Bed-and-Breakfast Workshops

Last year, the owner of a bed-and-breakfast in a nearby state invited me to present a workshop, garden lecture, and garden tour at her inn. I quickly agreed and supplied her with some information about myself. Soon thereafter, she sent me a brochure describing the inn's special weekend offerings, and I was delighted to see that I was listed among them.

The inn owner paid me a flat fee for my services and also allowed me to set up a sales display on one of her wide front porches. We held the workshop itself on the large, covered back porch, and the inn's gardens beyond served as illustrations for the herb-garden slide show I gave after the delightful herbal meal that the hostess served to her guests.

The participating ladies spent their first few minutes on the porch of this lovely Victorian inn. As they examined the many herbal craft items I'd brought along, I explained the "how-to" of each. The guests then paid their fees and proceeded to the back porch for the first part of my workshop, during which each guest made a tussie mussie while she learned about the Victorian "language of flowers" (see page 47).

Next, we carried our completed nosegays with us as we examined the herbs growing in the garden. As we walked, I explained each herb's common use and a bit of its history and lore. Then we washed up for the special herbal lunch, and what a lunch it was! Every bite was a delight to the eyes and palate.

Following lunch, we returned to the back porch, where, with my help, each guest followed a step-by-step procedure to make a large herbal wreath. I'd brought plenty of materials with me, so each lady was able to choose herbs and everlastings in colors she liked. All the completed wreaths were beautiful, and oddly enough, no two were similar, which surprised me because everyone in the workshop had used the same materials, and we'd all followed the same steps.

All in all, the weekend proved to be a delightful and profitable vacation for me. Giving workshops of this sort is an especially useful way to spread word of your skills when you don't have a shop of your own.

I made this window treatment for one of my customers, Julia, who had decorated her bedroom with handmade Austrian shades (pictured here), a maroon and pink bedspread, and a new Oriental rug. My job was to come up with a design that would coordinate both the colors in these materials, and the bare wood window frame, door, and baseboards. I selected a grapevine base to complement the wood, and delicate, complementary herb and flower colors to accentuate the very feminine decor.

Custom Interiors

I'm often approached by people who want a special herbal creation that's designed for their space in colors and herbs of their own choosing. At times, these customers even provide some of the herbs and everlastings that they'd like me to incorporate. I've made wreaths and swags for homes, bed-and-breakfast inns, restaurants, churches, and galleries. (On pages 104 and 115, you'll see two of these projects, which were photographed "on location.")

Start by visiting the site. While you're there, take note of the customer's decorating style and measure the area if necessary. (If the customer is ordering a wreath to fit above a fireplace, for example, measure from the top of the mantel to the ceiling.) Try to get some swatches of fabric that match the customer's curtain tiebacks or upholstery fabrics, so that you can match color tints and shades.

Remember that herbs often add fragrance as well as beauty to the environment. Be sure that your customer is familiar with the herbs that you intend to use and with their particular fragrances, as it's not unusual to run into people to whom particular odors just aren't appealing.

The next step is to agree upon a design. Provide the customer with an estimated price at this time so that she won't be surprised later! If she wishes the finished item to be delivered and installed, include your time and the cost of gasoline in your estimate. If you're going to install your own work, don't forget to bring a ladder.

Lectures with Refreshments

Another way to make money with your knowledge of herbs and herbal crafts is to give guest lectures at garden clubs, home-demonstration club meetings, public libraries, and community colleges. My favorite form of reimbursement for these talks is to have my basic expenses paid and to be allowed to set up my display of wreaths, potpourri, sachets, teas, vinegars, blends, books, and other herbal products for sale.

Find out how many people will be attending, where you'll be speaking, whether or not you'll have access to a refrigerator and freezer if you'd like to serve refreshments, and whether anyone will be available to help you. If you'll be setting up a display, be sure to find out how much floor space you'll have and whether you should bring your own tables. Try to visit the site in advance.

Prepare some Rose Geranium Pound Cake and Rosemary Punch (see the recipes on the next page) a day in advance.

On the day of your lecture, arrive at least one hour early. If you're setting up a display of goods for sale, bring three each of a range of products, from easy-to-make to very sophisticated. Be sure to wear your "costume."

As the guests arrive, pass out a sheet of paper for names and addresses; you'll add them to your office address file for future mailings. A door prize—unexpected and unannounced—is a great way to welcome people. Offer one of your products to the person whose birthday is closest to the day of the lecture!

While some of your audience members will be expert gardeners, others may have purchased their first parsley plants the day before. As you make your presentation, let the serious gardeners know that you, too, are continuing to learn about herbs, and let the beginners know that there's no such thing as a stupid question.

Divide your presentation into two "acts," with refreshments served at the intermission. Especially during evening presentations, audience members who have worked all day may be tired; a brief break will keep them from dozing off. Take this opportunity to distribute your business cards (and a brochure if you have one).

Over the years, I've collected a nice array of herb-garden slides, which I use as the basis for my talks. When possible, I also bring along living herb plants to "scratch and sniff"; most of these wind up in someone's garden. Many of the attendees later come out to see my gardens and shop. Whenever I give one of my herb talks, I feel as if I'm spreading the gospel of herbs: health and happiness!

ROSEMARY PUNCH

1 46-ounce (1.4 l) can unsweetened pineapple juice

8 sprigs rosemary, 3" (7.6 cm) long

1/2 cup sugar

Pinch of salt

1-1/2 cups lemon juice

2 cups water

One-liter bottle of sweet, carbonated lemon-lime drink

Heat one cup of the pineapple juice to boiling. Add the rosemary, sugar, and salt. Remove from heat and steep for ten minutes. Strain into a pitcher, using a tea strainer to catch the rosemary. Add the lemon juice, water, remaining pineapple juice, and a one-liter bottle of lemon-lime soda. Refrigerate until party time. Place some crushed ice or an herbal ice ring (see next recipe) in a punch bowl and pour the punch over the ice. Ladle into punch cups and await praise!

ICE RING

Fill a bundt cake pan with 1" (2.5 cm) of water and freeze. On top of the ice, arrange mint leaves, orange slices, and edible herb flowers such as nasturtiums, calendula, borage, and pinks. (Be sure you include only edible flowers!) Cover with water and freeze until party time.

ROSE GERANIUM POUND CAKE

1/2 pound (227 g) butter

1 cup sour cream

3 cups sugar

6 eggs

2 teaspoons vanilla

3 cups all-purpose flour

1/2 teaspoon salt

3/4 teaspoon double-acting baking powder

Spray-on cooking oil

Preheat the oven to 350°F (177°C). To prepare the pan, first coat it with spray-on cooking oil. (You may substitute grease and flour at this stage.) Place a waxed-paper template in the bottom of the pan and coat again with spray-on oil.

Cut five or six rose geranium (pelargonium) leaves and wash them gently in very hot water. Pat the leaves dry and remove any stem pieces. Arrange the dry leaves face down on top of the waxed paper. I place each leaf with its base next to the tube and its "fingers" pointed outward. To prevent them from baking into the cake batter, spray the leaves heavily with oil.

Mix the room-temperature ingredients in the order given, adding the eggs one at a time and sifting dry ingredients before mixing them in. Spoon the batter into a 10" (25.4 cm) tube pan, being careful not to disturb the leaves. Bake for 50 to 60 minutes.

The Projects

Making herbal craft projects is a challenge and a joy. In this section, you'll be given instructions for creating four different kinds of herbal products: culinary, fragrant, wedding, and decorative. These categories, as you'll see right away, sometimes overlap!

In most cases, the project instructions are intended to be guidelines only, which is why they don't often specify exactly how many stems to use or how long each stem should be. When a project is exceptionally complex, however, I've added more specifics.

If you're entirely new to wreath making, start by reviewing the basic wreath-making tips on the next page. Then make one of the wreath projects. Once you're comfortable with the general procedure, you'll see how easy it is to create your own style by substituting your favorite herbs.

Many of my products come with customer instruction cards, which provide advice on use or care. You'll see these cards in several of the projects that follow.

Gardening and crafting are natural progressions of my early life experiences. I've always enjoyed making things, and my earliest memories are visual. As a little girl, I created elaborate, fanciful environments from bits of broken mirror, moss, twigs, and flowers— environments that I thought would entice fairies to come and play while I slept. On bicycle excursions, I rode through neighborhood backyards so that I could look at ponds and gardens and smell the sweetness of roses and honeysuckle in the still heat of southern summer days. Life was a blessing to be embraced and enjoyed.

Wreath-Making Tips

❧ Use your imagination when selecting the type and size of your wreath base. Straw bases, vine bases, cardboard circles, and even the plastic lids of margarine containers will all work. The largest herb wreath I ever created was 56" (142 cm) in diameter; the smallest was about 1" (2.5 cm).

❧ To save time and energy and to reduce stress, assemble materials ahead of time.

❧ For easier handling and reduced shattering, always mist dry materials with water before you begin work.

❧ Wrap straw wreath bases with nylon or cotton tulle before applying herbs. Doing so will make the backs of your wreaths more attractive and will also prevent small slivers of straw from escaping. Use a floral pin to attach one end of the tulle to the base, but don't cut the tulle from its roll yet. Wind the roll around the base until the tulle overlaps the starting point slightly. Then cut the tulle from the roll and secure the free end with another floral pin.

❧ Apply materials to the inner rim of the base first, then to the outer rim, and finish by filling in the front surface.

❧ For a uniform and visually pleasing circular-wreath presentation, always apply your dried materials so that they run in the same direction around the wreath.

❧ Move the base in quarter turns as you complete sections.

❧ To protect dried materials from moisture and dust, spray the completed wreath with a fixative. Some people substitute hair spray, but I've found that the sticky sweetness of hair spray attracts insects.

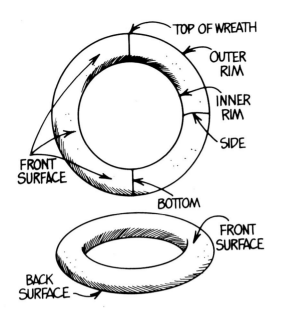

TOP OF WREATH

OUTER RIM

INNER RIM

SIDE

FRONT SURFACE

BOTTOM

FRONT SURFACE

BACK SURFACE

*T*he wreath project instructions in this book
make use of the part names provided here.

❧ Chenille stems make excellent wreath hangers when
threaded through the wreath base and twisted into loops.
The beauty here is that the wire's soft cover keeps it
from scratching walls and furniture. (I also use chenille
stems to attach garlands to banisters and nosegays to
glassware stems.)

❧ Keep finished wreaths away from direct sunlight to
prevent colors from fading. Be sure to add this information to your customer instruction cards, too.

Now kick off your shoes, make yourself a cup of herb
tea, curl up on your favorite sofa, and browse through
the projects that follow until you find the one you'd like
to make first. Have fun!

CULINARY PROJECTS

Sage Blossom Vinegar

These vinegars, so picturesque in the windowsill, would actually fare much better if they were kept in a pantry or refrigerator.

What You'll Need
(for six to nine bottles)

    Saucepan
    Funnel
    Sterilized bottles
    Handheld bottle capper and caps
    Labels

Project ingredients:

    Four to six 4" (10.2 cm) stems of sage blossoms
      per bottle
    1 gallon (3.8 l) 4% white vinegar

Time to Complete

Ten minutes per bottle for the first stage and no more than three days for the second

Method

1. When your sage is at bloom stage, pick the stems and wash them gently in warm water.

2. Place the stems in sterilized bottles.

3. Heat the vinegar just to boiling, and, using a funnel, add to cover the tops of the stems.

4. Cap the bottles and place them in a sunny window. Within a few days, you'll have a gorgeous best-seller—a pink vinegar that can be used to marinate meats or mixed with oils to make salad dressing.

5. Remove the bottles from the window to prevent breakdown of the contents.

6. Don't forget to label your vinegar before displaying it for sale.

To store your vinegar properly, keep it in a cool, dark place.

Culinary Gift Basket

This small gift basket presents Raspberry Herbal Vinegar, a bag of lavender accompanied by a recipe for Lavender Cookies, Chamomile and Peppermint Tea Bags, and several cinnamon sticks. Package this project in cellophane so that the contents will show and add a pretty bow with silk flowers and ivy tucked inside it.

(continued on next page)

Culinary Gift Basket (continued)

RASPBERRY VINEGAR
(for six to nine bottles)

What You'll Need

> Large-mouthed one-gallon (3.8 l) glass container with twist-on lid
>
> Saucepan
>
> Plastic wrap
>
> Labels
>
> Wire-mesh strainer with coffee filter inside
>
> Sterilized bottles
>
> Handheld bottle capper and caps
>
> Corks
>
> Tulle
>
> Raffia

Project ingredients:

> 2 pints (946 ml) raspberries
>
> 1 gallon (3.8 l) 4% white vinegar

Time to Complete

About one hour for the first stage and three to six weeks for the second

Method

1. In some locations, you may only make and bottle vinegars if your kitchen has met agency approval. Vinegars must also be clearly labeled with their names and ingredients. Before you begin, check with your local health department regarding compliance with these rules.

2. Gently wash the berries and place them into the large glass container.

3. Warm the vinegar just to the boiling point and then add to the berries to cover them. (I warm the vinegar two cups at a time in the microwave.)

4. To prevent the container lid from rusting, cover the top of the container with plastic wrap; then place a twist-on lid over the plastic.

5. Attach a temporary label which includes the date. Store in a dark place for three to six weeks.

6. Strain the vinegar through the coffee filter into a sterilized bottle and cap the bottle. Some of the fancy bottles available for herbal vinegars have necks that won't accept metal caps. On these, use corks instead and tie a pretty bow around the neck. If you use a

cap, wrap a cork in a small square of tulle and tie it to the bottle neck with a raffia bow.

7. Affix a permanent label.

If left in bright light for longer than a week, the berries have a tendency to break down and get mushy, so keep this bottle in the refrigerator or in a closed cupboard.

LAVENDER COOKIE RECIPE

> 1/2 cup unsalted butter
>
> 1 cup sugar
>
> 2 eggs
>
> 1/2 teaspoon vanilla extract
>
> 1 teaspoon dried lavender blossoms, finely chopped
>
> 1-1/2 cups all-purpose flour
>
> 2 teaspoons baking powder

Preheat oven to 375°F (191°C). In a medium bowl, cream the butter and sugar until light and fluffy. Beat in the eggs, vanilla, and lavender, and mix well. Combine the flour and baking powder and add to the lavender mixture. Stir until well blended. Drop by teaspoons onto an ungreased baking sheet and bake eight to ten minutes or until lightly browned around the edges. Let the cookies cool on the baking sheet for a minute or two before removing them. Enjoy alone or with vanilla ice cream or tea.

CHAMOMILE AND PEPPERMINT TEA BAGS

Many people, especially children, prefer herb teas that have only one or two flavors to teas with complex herbal blends. Chamomile or dried peppermint (as well as other mints) can be packaged in purchased tea bags, which are available from wholesale herb companies and at many health-food stores. The bags are filled and then sealed with a hot iron. To keep the filled bags clean, package them in plastic bags.

Herbal Butter Mix

*Your customers will love
flavoring their own butter with
this delicious herbal blend.
One of the ingredients,
lemon-juice powder,
is available at many health-
food stores, but if you have
trouble finding it, just add this line to the customer instruction card:
"For extra flavor, add a few drops of fresh lemon juice when mixing."*

What You'll Need

Mixing bowl and spoon
Measuring spoons
Electric coffee grinder or mortar and pestle
Plastic bag, zip-type

Project ingredients:

1 tablespoon chives
1 tablespoon basil
1 tablespoon parsley
1 tablespoon tarragon
1 tablespoon rosemary
1 tablespoon marjoram
1 teaspoon garlic powder
1/2 teaspoon lemon juice powder

Time to Complete

About 20 to 30 minutes

Method

1. Mix all the ingredients together, using a small electric coffee grinder if you have one available or a mortar and pestle if you don't.

2. Package in a small plastic bag.

Allow 1/2 pound (226.8 g) butter, margarine, or cream cheese to reach room temperature. Add one heaping teaspoon of the herbal blend and mix well. Use on top of steamed vegetables or on warm bread.

Warm your teapot by rinsing it with boiling water. Add one heaping teaspoon of tea for each person and an extra teaspoon "for the pot." Cover with boiling water and allow to steep for five minutes. Strain into cups. Use the cinnamon stick for stirring.

Feeling Good Tea Blend

Feeling Good Tea will help to tame an upset tummy, but don't wait till you're feeling bad to try some—it tastes great, too. Select attractive containers for all your teas and be sure to include a tea ball in each package.

What You'll Need

Mixing bowl and spoon
Measuring cup
Tin with lid
Tea ball
Cellophane
Ribbon or raffia
6" (15.2 cm) cinnamon stick

Feeling Good ingredients:

1 cup black peppermint
1 cup spearmint
1/2 cup lemon grass

Time to Complete

If all the ingredients, tins, and packaging materials have been set out on your work surface, you can make up about a dozen containers of tea in one and one-half hours.

What to Do

1. Blend the ingredients together well.

2. To protect the tea from sunlight, which will cause its colors to fade, package it in an attractive, airtight tin.

3. Wrap the tin in cellophane, along with a tea ball and a customer instruction card.

4. Tie the package closed with a ribbon or raffia bow, inserting a 6"-long cinnamon stick in the bow.

Spicy Mint Tea Blend

Tea blends are easy-to-package, dependable sellers. Let your customers know that the herbs in this one will their lift spirits and warm their souls.

What You'll Need

Mixing bowl and spoon
Measuring cup
Tin with lid
Tea ball
Cellophane
Ribbon or raffia
6" (15.2 cm) cinnamon stick

Spicy Mint ingredients:

1 cup spearmint
1 cup orange peel pieces, cut small
1 cup cinnamon chips, cut small
1/4 cup cardamom, ground
1 vanilla bean, slit lengthwise and finely chopped

Time to Complete

Once you're organized, about 10 minutes apiece or less

What to Do

1. Blend the ingredients together well.

2. To protect the tea from sunlight, which will cause its colors to fade, package it in an attractive, airtight tin.

3. Wrap the tin in cellophane, along with a tea ball, and a customer instruction card.

4. Tie the package closed with a ribbon or raffia bow, inserting a 6"-long cinnamon stick in the bow.

Add honey or sugar and orange or lemon slices as desired; use the cinnamon stick for stirring. During cold weather, create "comfort food" by adding a couple of cloves, a few allspice berries, a sliver of candied ginger, a few rose hips, and a small chunk of cinnamon.

Spicy Hot Pad

Placed under a steaming teapot or hot casserole, the Spicy Hot Pad not only protects your table top from damaging heat but also releases a delightful herbal aroma.

To help retain its fragrance, store this pad in a plastic bag when not in use. To reactivate aroma, crush contents by striking the pad several times with a hammer.

What You'll Need

Scissors
Sewing machine or needle and thread
Iron and ironing board
Mixing bowl
Measuring cup
Spoon
Plastic bag, zip-type

Project materials:

Two 8" by 8" (20.3 by 20.3 cm) pieces of fabric
1 cup cinnamon chips, cut small
1 cup anise seeds
1 cup whole cloves
1 cup nutmeg pieces
1 cup allspice berries
1 cup rosemary needles

Time to Complete

Making one pad will take 25 to 30 minutes. Practice and repetition will help you pick up speed.

Method

1. Place the pieces of fabric on top of one another, with their right sides facing in.

2. Stitch three of the sides closed, placing the seams about 1/2" (1.3 cm) from the edges.

3. Turn the partly stitched square right side out. At the open fourth side, fold the fabric edges down and in to create a square that is roughly 7" by 7" (17.8 by 17.8 cm). Press the folds with an iron.

4. Create three "tunnels" of equal width, each with one open end, by stitching three parallel lines down the square.

5. Combine the spice-mix ingredients, blending them well.

6. To complete the pad, fill the tunnels with the spice mix until they're at least 1" thick. Top-stitch the open edge to seal it.

7. Package the finished pads in plastic bags to show off the colorful fabric.

Seasoning Gift Basket

This tiny handwoven basket contains one bottle of Salad Sprinkles and one of Herbes de Provence, both favorite culinary blends of my customers. One woman who buys Salad Sprinkles from me adds a dash to her toast-with-cottage-cheese each morning!

You'll need to purchase some of these ingredients in bulk from wholesalers.

What You'll Need

Glue gun and glue

Gift basket

Excelsior

2 small jars (one glass and one plastic, to prevent breakage)

Cellophane

Raffia

Label

Recipe sheet

Salad Sprinkles ingredients:

1 tablespoon sesame seeds, toasted

1 tablespoon bell pepper flakes

1 tablespoon celery flakes

1 tablespoon chervil

1 tablespoon green onion flakes

1/2 teaspoon black pepper

1/4 teaspoon garlic powder

Herbes de Provence ingredients:

1 tablespoon basil

1 tablespoon rosemary

1 tablespoon savory

1 tablespoon French tarragon

1 tablespoon thyme   *(continued on next page)*

Seasoning Gift Basket (continued)

Time to Complete

About one-half hour if the ingredients are assembled in advance

Method

1. Mix each set of ingredients together.

2. Package each mix in a small jar.

3. Fill the bottom of the basket with excelsior.

4. Roll up a recipe sheet (see below), tie it with raffia, and place it, along with the jars, into the basket. By all means substitute your own recipes if you like.

5. Wrap the filled basket with cellophane, and glue on a raffia bow and label.

RECIPE FOR REALLY GOOD BLACK BEAN SOUP

2 cups black beans
1/2 cup olive oil
1 large onion, chopped
1 cup celery, chopped
1 4-ounce (114 g) jar pimentos
Dash of red wine
1 clove garlic, minced
1 tablespoon sugar
1/2 teaspoon salt
1 tablespoon Herbes de Provence

Place the beans in a soup pot, cover with water, and bring to a boil. Remove from heat and let stand for one hour. Drain. Cover with cold water and add remaining ingredients. Cook over medium heat until beans are tender. Serve with a dollop of sour cream.

Salad Sprinkles: Shake over garden salads or scrambled eggs.

Herbes de Provence: Use in soups and stews.

Mug Mats

These mug mats, which are similar to Spicy Hot Pads (page 62), sell well in packages of four. Fill them with the same spice mix used in that project, or mix up your own fragrant version.

What You'll Need

(for each mat)

Scissors
Sewing machine or needle and thread
Iron and ironing board
Mixing bowl
Spoon
Ribbon
6" cinnamon stick
Cellophane bag

Project materials

One 5" by 5" (12.7 by 12.7 cm) square of closely woven fabric
One 5" by 5" square of quilted cotton fabric
Spice mix from Spicy Hot Pad project or Citrus & Spice potpourri (page 67)

Time to Complete

Making a set of four takes about one hour.

Method

1. Place one piece of fabric on top of the other, wrong sides facing out.

2. Stitch three of the edges together, locating the seam about 1/4" (.6 cm) from the edges.

3. Turn the mat right side out and fold the open edges down and in. Press the seams with an iron.

4. Fill the mat with the Spicy Hot Pad mix or with Citrus & Spice potpourri that's been chopped into finer pieces. The mat should now be about 1/2" (1.3 cm) thick.

5. Close the mat by top-stitching along its open edge.

6. To package the mats for sale, tie four of them together with matching or contrasting ribbon. Tuck a 6" (15.2 cm) cinnamon stick under the ribbon and enclose the mats in a cellophane bag tied with a ribbon bow to match the ribbon inside.

When placed under mugs of hot tea or coffee, these mats will not only protect your table, they'll also release a fragrant spice scent. Can be used at home or office. To reactivate aroma, crush contents by striking mat with a hammer.

Potpourri

The fragrances, colors, and textures of many dried herbs and flowers may be incorporated in potpourri. Shown in the photo to the left are three marketable recipes: Queen's Garden (left), Citrus & Spice (top), and Rose Garden (right). Let your customers know that the Citrus & Spice mixture also makes an excellent simmer (see photo below).

To make smaller amounts, just decrease the pound measurements to cups. All three recipes are mixed in a similar fashion (Steps 1 through 3), but the instructions that follow also note slight variations.

What You'll Need

Large container for mixing
Spoon
Large storage containers with lids

Queen's Garden materials:

1 pound (454 g) lavender flowers
1 pound red rose petals and flowers
1 pound rosemary needles
1 pound hibiscus flower pods
1/2 pound (227 g) orange peel pieces
3 tablespoons orris root granules (optional)
30 drops high-quality rose oil (optional)

Citrus & Spice materials:

1 pound cut bay leaves
1 pound rosemary needles
1 pound star anise
1 pound allspice berries
1 pound whole cloves
1 pound cinnamon chips
1/4 pound (113 g) nutmeg pieces
1/4 pound sassafras pieces
1 pound orange peel
1/2 pound grapefruit peel
1 pound lemon peel

Rose Garden materials:

1 pound red rose blooms
1 pound red rose petals
1 pound pink rose blooms and petals
1 pound whole rose hips
3 tablespoons orris root granules (optional)
30 to 40 drops high-quality rose oil (optional)

Time to Complete

Forty minutes to an hour to mix all three

Basic Method

1. Mix all the dried ingredients together.

2. If you'd like a headier fragrance in your Queen's Garden or Rose Garden potpourri, add the optional orris root and oil.

3. Store in a covered glass or plastic container away from light. (Don't use metal containers, which will cause the oils to become rancid.)

(continued on next page)

Potpourri (continued)

Variations

Rose Garden: Blend the root and scent oil first, and then blend with the potpourri by placing all the ingredients in a glass jar with lid. Shake the jar or stir the contents thoroughly once a day for two weeks.

Citrus & Spice: Allow the mixed ingredients to "marry" for one week before offering this potpourri for sale. This potpourri may be simmered if desired. Just add these lines to your customer instruction card: "Place two cups of water in a small saucepan or slow cooker, and sprinkle about 1/4 cup of the potpourri on top. Bring to a boil; then reduce the heat to a simmer. Reuse until no fragrance remains. Never let the pot boil dry!"

Display your potpourri in ceramic, clay, or glass bowls, or in baskets. Never place in metal containers, which may interact with the oils.

Pamper-Yourself Fragrant Gift Basket

Encourage your customers to pamper themselves with the wonderful items tucked inside this purple basket: a Lavender Dryer Sachet (page 70), a Lavender Sachet Bag, a Lavender Lovely, a bar of Lavender Soap, and an Herbal Bath Refresher. For a truly regal look, drape some lace over the edge of the basket, wrap the basket with cellophane, and tie it off with a bow in shades of lavender or purple.

LAVENDER SACHET BAG

This particular sachet bag, made with white flannel, has old lace whipped around its upper edges and a white velvet ribbon tied around a small satin rose. To make the bag, follow the instructions on page 76.

LAVENDER LOVELIES

These are easier to make than traditional lavender wands, but they smell just as wonderful!

What You'll Need
(for one Lovely)

> Scissors

Project materials:

> 12 stems fresh lavender
> Lavender tulle
> Satin ribbon

Time to Complete

Ten to fifteen minutes each

Method

1. Wrap the lavender stems in a length of tulle.

2. Tie the base with a satin ribbon bow.

3. Rest the project in a flat position for three to five days or until the stems and blooms have dried.

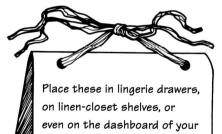

Place these in lingerie drawers, on linen-closet shelves, or even on the dashboard of your automobile.

LAVENDER SOAP

This soap, which I purchase rather than make, is extremely gentle on the skin. Wrap each bar in a square of lavender tulle and tie it closed with a satin ribbon. A 6" (15.2 cm) length of pearls and a silk flower add the finishing touches.

HERBAL BATH REFRESHER

Because it gets wet in your bath water, this project is offered in a cotton, drawstring bag which can be suspended as it dries. Make the bag just as you would make one for the Lavender Dryer Sachet on the next page.

What You'll Need
(for one bag)

    Mixing bowl and spoon
    Measuring spoon
    Plastic bag, zip-type

Project materials:

    1 heaping tablespoon rosemary, to relieve tired limbs

    1 heaping tablespoon lavender, to act as a natural disinfectant

    1 heaping teaspoon pennyroyal, to comfort the nerves

    1 heaping teaspoon lemon balm, to relax

    1 heaping teaspoon chamomile, to soothe

(continued on next page)

Pamper-Yourself Fragrant Gift Basket (continued)

Project materials (continued)

    1 heaping teaspoon mint, to refresh

    1" (2.5 cm) quick-cooking oatmeal,
       to soften the skin

    3 bay leaves, to comfort aching limbs

    (If you need more herbs to fill the bag,
       use lavender or chamomile.)

    Drawstring bag

    Cotton ball

    Yellow ribbon

Time to Complete

Once the bag is completed, five to eight minutes

1. Mix the herbal ingredients thoroughly.

2. Fill the drawstring bag with the mixture, topping it off with a cotton ball to keep the herbs from escaping.

3. Pull the drawstring closed and tie the ends in a double knot.

4. Double-knot the drawstring around a yellow-ribbon bow. When packaging these products for sale individually, enclose each one in a plastic bag and add a label that provides ingredients and directions.

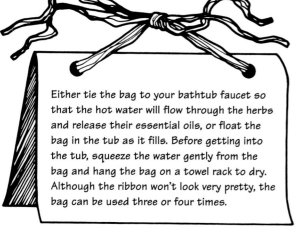

Either tie the bag to your bathtub faucet so that the hot water will flow through the herbs and release their essential oils, or float the bag in the tub as it fills. Before getting into the tub, squeeze the water gently from the bag and hang the bag on a towel rack to dry. Although the ribbon won't look very pretty, the bag can be used three or four times.

Lavender Dryer Sachet

This easy-to-make dryer sachet continues to be one of my best-selling items. Although I first used it exclusively with lingerie, I was soon placing it in the clothes dryer with bed linens and towels, too. When my younger son came home from school happily claiming that people were stopping him in the hallways to sniff his shirts, I realized that I'd neglected to remove the sachet from the dryer before I put in his clothes. From that day forth, we scented all our wearables with lavender!

What You'll Need

    Scissors

    Sewing machine or needle and thread

    Iron and ironing board

    Blunt-tipped tapestry needle

    Plastic bag, zip-type

    Label

Project materials:

    One 11" by 3-3/4" (27.9 by 9.5 cm) piece
       of cotton fabric

    Cotton string

    3/4 cup lavender buds

    1 cotton ball

    8" by 1-1/2" (20.3 by 3.8 cm) lavender ribbon

Time to Complete

Once the bag is made, five to eight minutes

Method

1. Place the fabric in front of you, wrong side up. Fold the short edges over about 1/4".

2. Press the folds with an iron and stitch these seams down.

3. Fold the fabric in half, right sides facing in, and stitch the two long edges closed, making the seams about 1/4" from the edges of the fabric.

4. Turn the bag right side out. At the open end, use your tapestry needle to thread the cotton string through the seam. The string will need to enter the seam, then exit and reenter it in order to bypass the seam on the long edge, and finally, exit once again.

5. Fill the bag with as many lavender buds as possible. Pack the lavender tightly, as the buds will shrink from the heat of the dryer.

6. Place the cotton ball on top of the buds to keep them from escaping when they shrink.

7. Pull the drawstring tightly closed, and tie the ends in a double knot to secure the bag's contents.

8. Make a bow by folding the ribbon in thirds. Place it across the drawstring knot and tie it securely with the ends of the string.

9. To package, place the bag in a labeled plastic bag with an instruction card bearing your logo.

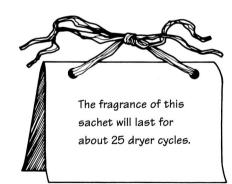

The fragrance of this sachet will last for about 25 dryer cycles.

Catnip Cuties

While these winsome sachets may not impress your customers with their fragrance, they'll certainly impress your customers' cats! I make my Cuties with suede, but any closely woven material will work. Just remember that felines will treat these treats roughly, so the fabric will have to stand up to wear and tear.

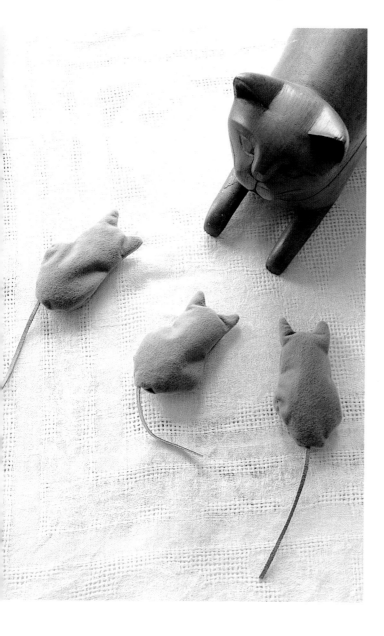

What You'll Need

(for one Cutie)

    Sewing machine or needle and thread
    Pencil
    Scissors

Project materials:

    Two 3" by 5" (7.6 by 12.7 cm) pieces of fabric
    Heavy paper or cardboard
    3" (7.6 cm) strip of leather
    Dried catnip

Time to Complete

Depending on your sewing expertise, 20 to 30 minutes

Method

1. On the paper or cardboard, draw a pattern for a cat, making it no larger than either piece of fabric. Cut this pattern out.
2. Using the pattern, cut the two pieces of fabric to size.
3. Place the pieces of fabric on top of each other, right sides in.
4. Stitch around the outer edges, leaving a 1" (2.5 cm) opening at the tail end.
5. Turn the fabric cat right side out, using a pencil or knitting needle to help turn the ears inside out.
6. Fill the cat with catnip, insert the tail in the opening, and stitch the opening closed.

Potpourri Baskets

After the cellophane wrapping is removed, these baskets may be placed anywhere in the house to impart their delightful fragrance. The baskets are filled with spicy apple potpourri.

Note that the apple slices are dried in an electric dehydrator.

What You'll Need

Cellophane

Raffia

Cinnamon sticks

Strawflowers and rudbeckia blooms

Glue gun and glue

Project materials:

Several dried apple slices

Small baskets

1 cup hemlock cones

1 cup cinnamon chips

1 cup sage leaves

1 cup rose petals

1 cup of 1" (2.5 cm) cinnamon stick pieces

1 cup rosemary needles

1 cup apple pieces

1 cup chamomile flowers

1 cup juniper berries

1 cup tilia flowers

1 cup white yarrow heads, broken into
   tiny florets

1 cup whole cloves

1/2 cup orris root granules

30 drops apple-and-cinnamon oil

Time to Complete

Forty-five minutes to an hour

Method

1. Mix the potpourri ingredients together. (Store in a covered jar, away from direct sunlight.)

2. To package for sale, fill a small straw basket with potpourri and top with dried apple slices.

3. Wrap the basket in cellophane; then tie the cellophane closed with a raffia bow, leaving streamers on the ends.

4. Hot-glue a dried apple slice and a cinnamon stick over the bow. Finish with a red strawflower and a yellow rudbeckia bloom or other decorative blooms.

Sylvan Potpourri in Clay Saucers

Because this potpourri isn't hidden inside a sachet bag, the colors and shapes of its aromatic herbs and spices should be attractive and eye-catching. As you can see, the pieces are quite large.

What You'll Need

Large mixing container
Spoon
Cellophane
Raffia
Several 3" (7.6 cm) cinnamon sticks

Project materials:

Several 6" (15.3 cm) clay saucers
1 cup whole bay leaves
1 cup rose hips
1 cup orange or red globe amaranth heads
1 cup dried rudbeckia blooms
1 cup allspice berries
1 cup whole star anise
1 cup cinnamon chips, with some 2" (5.1 cm) sticks included
1 cup whole cloves
1 cup whole nutmeg
1 cup nutmeg pieces
1 cup orange peel
1 cup small hemlock cones
1 cup whole rosemary needles
1 cup sandalwood chips

Time to Complete

About 30 minutes if ingredients are assembled in advance

Method

1. Mix the potpourri ingredients thoroughly.

2. Fill each clay saucer with potpourri.

3. To package, wrap each saucer in a pouf of cellophane; then tie the cellophane closed with a raffia bow, inserting a stick of cinnamon into the bow.

Citrus Sachet Bags

You may use any potpourri recipe to fill these sachets, but try to select one with a fragrance that will complement the decorative cinnamon sticks and orange slices.

What You'll Need

(for one sachet)

> Scissors
> Sewing machine or needle and thread
> Iron and ironing board
> Plastic bag, zip-type

Project materials:

> 7-1/2" by 10-1/2" (19.1 by 26.7 cm) piece of tightly woven fabric
> Potpourri (page 67)
> Cotton ball
> Rubber band
> Five 6" (15.2 cm) cinnamon sticks
> Tasseled jute or raffia cord
> Dried orange slice

Time to Complete

About 15 to 20 minutes

Method

1. Fold the fabric in half, right side facing in, to make a 7-1/2" by 5-1/4" (19.1 by 13.3 cm) rectangle.
2. Close one long edge and one short edge by stitching a seam 1/4" (.6 cm) from the edges of the fabric.
3. Turn the bag right side out. Fold the top edges of the bag in and down about 1-1/4" (3.2 cm) and press with an iron.
4. Fill the bag to about 1" (2.5 cm) from its top with any combination of herbs, spices, and citrus to suit your fancy.
5. Insert the cinnamon sticks into the opening in the bag.
6. To keep the potpourri inside, top it with a cotton ball and close the bag securely with a rubber band.
7. To disguise the rubber band, tie a jute or raffia bow over it.
8. Hot-glue the dried orange slice onto the fabric as shown in the photo.
9. Package in a plastic bag to keep the fabric clean.

Sachet Bags

Sachet bags may be made from any tightly woven material, including silk, cotton, or flannel. Antique handkerchiefs and circles of satin make your offerings most elegant. To make small sachets (and to save on hemming), use pinking shears to cut circles instead of rectangles; a pie plate makes a great template for cutting these.

What You'll Need
(for one rectangular sachet)

> Scissors
> Sewing machine or needle and thread
> Iron and ironing board
> Plastic bag, zip-type

Project materials:

> 8" by 9" (20.3 by 22.9 cm) piece of fabric
> Any potpourri blend (page 67)
> Cotton ball
> Rubber band
> Ribbon bow

Time to Complete

Thirty to forty minutes to make several

Method

1. Making the cloth bag is easy. Fold the material in half lengthwise, right side facing in.
2. Close one short end and one long edge by stitching a seam.
3. Turn the bag right side out. Then fold the narrow open end of the bag down and in about 2" (5.1 cm). Press the fold with an iron.
4. Fill the bag with potpourri to within 1-1/2" (3.8 cm) of the folded end. Place the cotton ball in the opening and secure the top with a tightly twisted rubber band. Finish the bag by tying a ribbon bow over the rubber band.
5. Package in plastic bags to keep the fabric clean.

Tuck sachets into lingerie or sweater drawers, hang them on hangers in your closets, suspend them from door-knobs, or hide them under chair and sofa cushions.

The projects in this section were photographed at an actual herbal wedding, about 20 minutes before the ceremony took place. They're presented here in the order that you might see them if you were a wedding guest, not in the order in which I made or arranged them.

Wedding Cake Embellishments

The cake arrived at the reception in its pristine, all-white state, preassembled and covered with icing scallops. My job was to add the herbal embellishments and cake topper, which I'd prepared in my own kitchen the night before and had packed very carefully with tissue in flat, lidded boxes. I also made an ivy base to be placed on the table around the wedding cake.

What You'll Need

> Scissors
> Glue gun and glue sticks
> Boxes with lids

Cake-Decoration materials:

> Flat sheets of semirigid plastic
> Oasis igloo flower holder
> Satin leaves
> Baby's breath
> Lavender
> Roses
> Mountain mint leaves (for topper)
> Springerai fern
> White larkspur
> Anise hyssop
> Oregano blooms

Ivy Base materials:

> Ivy
> Vegetable oil
> Crocheted Hearts (page 93)

Time to Complete

There's never enough time for on-site wedding work, so do as much as you can beforehand. With all materials assembled, the small decorations that encircle the tops of the lower cake layers take about five minutes each to create. The topper and ivy base each take about 45 minutes.

Method

(for lower levels of cake)

1. Cut off the wire stems from the satin leaves.
2. Onto each leaf, hot-glue some baby's breath, lavender, and a rose.
3. Store the decorated leaves in a box with a lid. When you reach the wedding site, arrange them on the cake as shown in the photograph on page 77.

Method

(for cake topper)

1. Ask the caterer for the diameter of the top cake layer. Don't rely on the bride to do this; make the call yourself!
2. Mark a circle of this diameter on the semirigid plastic and cut it out. (I use recycled plastic, washed and dried, from the bottom of bacon packages.) This circle will serve as a base and will actually fit directly on top of the iced cake layer.
3. Hot-glue the igloo flower holder in the center of the plastic circle.
4. Insert sprigs of fern, 2" to 4" (5.1 to 10.2 cm) long, all over the igloo holder to create a feathery background for your flowers.
5. Establish the height of the arrangement with white larkspur and roses.
6. Complete the arrangement by adding the anise hyssop and oregano blooms, remembering to balance colors, lines, forms, and textures.
7. Store the topper in a covered box until the wedding day.

Method

(for ivy base)

1. Prepare the fresh ivy by gathering it the day before the event and washing it with soapy water to remove any dirt and insects.
2. When the ivy has dried, gently rub the leaves with vegetable oil spray; this will make them shiny so that they'll reflect all available light.
3. Wrap the ivy around the base of the cake and arrange Crocheted Hearts among the leaves.

Over-the-Door Garland

One of the most striking features of this chapel is the set of carved entry doors, which depicts scenes from the Old and New Testaments. The bride requested that my decorations call the attention of out-of-town guests to these treasures.

My first step was to purchase a 16'-long (4.9 m) plumosa-fern garland, which I wired in place over the double doors. Then, as my helper and friend Beth stood on the ladder and wired small nosegays into the garland, I stood on the walkways creating more. The large bow at the very top of the garland is satin; smaller tulle bows hold the Crocheted Bells (page 92) in place at the garland's ends and peak.

(continued on next page)

Over-the-Door Garland (continued)

What You'll Need

Wire cutters

Scissors

Glue gun and glue sticks

Hammer

Nails

Project materials:

Plumosa-fern garland

Floral wire

Baby's breath

Lavender

Roses

Rubber bands

Floral tape

Satin ribbon, wide

Tulle

6 Crocheted Bells

Time to Complete

For an efficient team of two, about one hour

Method

1. Hammer three nails into the door frame to support the floral wire that will bear the weight of the garland. Center one nail above the doors and place the other two at the upper corners.

2. Wire the garland onto the nails securely so that the wind won't blow it down.

3. Make a large white satin bow and wire it in place at the peak of the garland.

4. Make small herbal nosegays, securing the stem ends of each with a tightly twisted rubber band. Cover the rubber bands with floral tape for easy insertion.

5. Wire the nosegays onto the garland, spacing them evenly and making sure to create the two halves of the garland as mirror images of one another.

6. Make three tulle bows. Using wire, attach two Crocheted Bells to each bow; then attach the bows to the ends and peak of the garland.

Garland for Bridal Registry

When you do an herbal wedding, take the Girl Scout motto to heart: Be prepared! You never know what last-minute requests will be made of you. At this wedding, which took place about three hours from my studio and gardens, the bride met me at the church carrying the guest register (a gift) in her arms. She wanted me to find some way to use it in the church vestibule!

First, I found a lectern there and placed the register on it. Next, I needed to whip up a decorative garland. A quick search of the grounds revealed a few evergreen trees. Some judicious pruning yielded several handfuls of evergreen tips, each about 10" (25.4 cm) long. (Ancient lore has it that hemlock protects the bearer from evil, so I guessed these greens would fit right into my wedding theme!) I salvaged a rope from under a seat in my van and some dried herbs from my emergency store; then I settled right down to assemble this project.

What You'll Need

Scissors

Wire cutters

Project materials:

30" (76.2 cm) piece of rope

Rubber bands

Floral spool wire

6" to 12" (15.2 to 30.5 cm) sprigs of:

Hemlock

Baby's breath

Oregano

Lavender

Globe amaranth

Statice

Pearly everlasting

Crocheted Bell (page 92)

Tulle bow

Time to Complete

About an hour

Method

1. Gather several small bouquets, using hemlock, baby's breath, oregano blooms, lavender, globe amaranth, statice, and pearly everlasting.

2. Cut the stem ends of the bouquets to even lengths and secure each one with a tightly twisted rubber band.

3. Using floral wire, attach the bouquets to the rope, disguising each wired bouquet end under the loose end of the next bouquet.

4. As an added embellishment, fasten a Crocheted Bell and a large tulle bow to the top of the garland.

Wedding Wreaths

I made two of these wreaths—one for each of the two chapel doors—to welcome guests into the sanctuary. After the wedding, the bride took them home as fragrant reminders of her most special day. The wreaths were made with herbs that are traditionally related to love and romance.

What You'll Need

(for one wreath)

Scissors

Glue gun and glue sticks

Chenille stem

Project materials:

16" (40.6 cm) straw wreath base

Tulle

Floral picks and pins

Silver king artemisia

Green herbs: ivy, mountain mint, peppermint, thyme, santolina, sweet Annie artemisia, bay leaves, salad burnet, spearmint, tarragon, and savory

Anise hyssop

Lavender

Baby's breath

Pinks

White statice sinuata

Globe amaranth

Oregano

Yarrow

Pearly everlasting

Powis castle artemisia

Crested celosia

Chamomile

Caspia

Rosemary

Sage

Three red roses to symbolize perfect love (the Father, the Son, and the Holy Ghost)

Time to Complete

About two hours

Method

1. Make a wreath hanger by slipping a chenille stem through the back of the wreath base and twisting it to make a secure loop.

2. Attach picks to several bunches of silver king artemisia; then pick the bunches around the inner and outer rims of the base.

3. Using fern pins here and in all succeeding steps, insert the green herbs around the outer rim, on top of the artemisia.

4. Insert anise hyssop and lavender, alternating them at 4" (10.2 cm) intervals around the front surface of the wreath.

5. Add the baby's breath at evenly spaced intervals.

6. Fill in the front surface of the wreath form with the remaining flowers and herbs, setting the three roses aside.

7. Attach picks to the three red roses and insert them into the top front wreath surface. (In the photo, you can see them peeking out just above the inner rim of the wreath.)

Pew Decorations

In order to facilitate seating at the wedding ceremony, decorations are attached to the rows of chapel chairs (or pews) that will be occupied by close relatives of the bride and groom. Note how the Crocheted Bells (page 92) have been incorporated into the design.

What You'll Need
(for one decoration)

Glue gun and glue sticks

Scissors

Project materials:

Tulle

Satin ribbon

Chenille stems

Floral wire

Plastic pew clip

2 Crocheted Bells

Springerai fern

Pink larkspur

Baby's breath

Pink yarrow

Oregano blooms

Pink statice sinuata

White statice sinuata

Lavender

Roses

(continued on next page)

Pew Decorations (continued)

Time to Complete

About one and one-half hours each

Method

1. Create a tulle bow with streamers of satin attached and wire it to the pew clip.

2. With the chenille stems, make hanging loops for the Crocheted Bells; then use them to wire the two bells onto the pew clip over the bow knot. Spread the bells apart so that flowers can be placed between them.

3. Form a bouquet of ferns and flowers, massing heavier looking materials at the bottom and layering additional materials on top so that blooms will point upward between the bells.

4. Use a chenille stem to wire the flowers in place between the bells.

5. Hot-glue a satin bow over the design to hide the chenille stem.

6. Fill any holes by hot-gluing other flowers into the design.

7. To prevent damage to these florals, store and transport them as follows:

   For each set of two arrangements, find a cardboard box with high walls.

   Clip one arrangement to one wall of the box, with its flowers inside the box cavity.

   Clip the other arrangement onto the opposite wall, also with its flowers inside the box cavity.

8. At the church, remove the arrangements from the boxes and mist them with water before attaching them to the backs of the pews or chairs. Be sure to place them close to the aisles.

I created these altar florals just a few hours before the wedding ceremony, while I stood on a breezeway between the chapel and reception site. I'd gathered flowers and herbs from my gardens that very morning, so herbal fragrance perfumed the church. Here, I'm placing mountain mint and ferns into the floral foam in plastic liners to establish the height, width, and line of the finished product. What a joy it was to drop cut-off stem ends and stripped leaves onto the cement walkway and not bother with them until after the work was completed!

Altar Arrangements in Wicker Baskets

Two of these floral arrangements were placed on either side of the very modern altar (see page 44). They were designed to repeat the colors in the stained glass window above and to complement the color of the bridesmaid's gown.

What You'll Need

Sharp knife

Bucket of water

Scissors

Wire cutters

Project materials:

Plastic liners

Oasis floral foam

Floral wire

Wicker baskets

Green herbs: mountain mint, sweet Annie artemisia, basil, tangerine southernwood, fern, ivy, and angelica

Anise hyssop

Baby's breath

Caspia

Cleome

Daisy fleabane

Feverfew

Joe-pye weed

Lavender

Bee balm (monarda)

Oregano

Pearly everlasting

Phlox

Purple coneflower

Queen Anne's lace

Rose

Rudbeckia

Silver king artemisia

Silver queen artemisia

Statice sinuata

Yarrow

Time to Complete

About two and one-half hours for two baskets—and I was praying the entire time that I'd get them done and into the sanctuary on time!

Method

1. Place a plastic liner in each wicker basket.

2. Cut pieces of oasis floral foam to fit inside the liners; then place them in the liners and cover them with water.

3. Start your arrangements by inserting the green herbs at the top, back, and front of each design.

4. Add the remaining herbs until the arrangement resembles an English cottage garden.

5. Mist the completed floral arrangements with water and carefully move them into place.

"Throw-Away" Bouquet and Bridal Bouquet

After the ceremony, the bride throws her bouquet, and the unmarried female guest who catches it is the one who will marry next—or so tradition would have us believe! This bouquet (pictured on the left) was sturdily constructed to withstand its flight and the crush of eager hands on landing; I used liberal amounts of hot glue.

The bridal bouquet, which is somewhat larger, has baby's breath knotted into its ribbon streamers. At the bride's request, I incorporated "something old,"—the small covered Bible which her mother had carried down the aisle years ago. Although you can't see it in the photo, the Bible is attached to the bouquet with rubber bands, which are covered with attractive ribbon. The bow and ribbon streamers were picked into the bouquet so that when the bride held the Bible, they would present themselves correctly to the guests and photographers. The use of picks and rubber bands allows the bride to detach the Bible and reverse the position of the bow and ribbons on the bouquet after the ceremony.

What You'll Need

Glue gun and glue sticks

Scissors

Floral picks

Purchased bouquet holder with Sahara foam

Purchased lace cuff for holder

White floral tape

Throw-Away Bouquet materials:

Satin corsage leaves

Sweet Annie artemisia

Caspia

Pearly everlasting

Lavender

White statice sinuata

Larkspur

Roses

White satin ribbon

Bridal Bouquet materials:

Materials for Throw-Away Bouquet

Anise hyssop

Rosemary

Silver king artemisia

White yarrow

Baby's breath

Time to Complete

About one and one-half to two hours each

Method

1. Attach the lace cuff to the bouquet holder, using floral tape to fasten the ends.

2. Before adding any materials, wrap the holder handle with 1"-wide (2.5 cm) white satin ribbon. Begin by tying a knot at the top of the handle, just under the cuff. Cut a 5"-long (12.7 cm) ribbon tail at one end, but leave the remaining ribbon on the spool. Wrap the handle by spiraling the spool downward around it, in the direction of the tail. Every second or third turn around the handle, flip the ribbon over so that its opposite surface faces up before continuing to wind. Wind to the bottom, add a drop or two of hot glue where necessary, and wind back up to cover the first wrap. Cut to leave another 5" tail and knot above the first tail.

3. Make a white satin bow and use the two tails to tie it in place. (The placement of this bow on top of the handle and behind the visible portion of the bouquet should help a nervous bride ascertain the top of her bouquet by touch, and the ribbon will accommodate her sweaty palms.) As an added touch, I often use a gold-ink pen to write the first name of the bride and groom and the wedding date on the back top surface of the bouquet holder.

4. Cut the wire stems of several green satin corsage leaves to 2" (5.1 cm) lengths. To make a continuous circular background, use your glue gun to attach the leaves around the perimeter of the bouquet holder; they should touch at the sides.

5. Between the leaves, insert and glue 4" to 5" (10.2 to 12.7 cm) lengths of sweet Annie and silver king artemisia.

6. Pick and insert baby's breath over the other materials. (In the Throw-Away Bouquet, use sturdy caspia instead.)

7. Continue to work in the flowers and greenery, moving from the outer rim of the bouquet towards the center, alternating colors and textures and adding baby's breath or caspia here and there. As you move towards the traditional rose at the center, bring materials forward (make the stems longer) in order to achieve a rounded effect.

8. When you reach the center of the bouquet, form a small nosegay (including the rose) in your hand. Attach a pick to the nosegay, insert the pick into the bouquet, and secure it with a drop of hot glue.

9. To make the picked bow for the bridal bouquet, first form the bow, using at least eight loops of ribbon. Then wire a pick to it.

10. Form a set of tails by knotting together three ribbons of varying lengths and attaching a pick at the knotted end.

11. Pick these tails into the bottom of the bouquet, between the lace cuff and satin leaves. Then insert the picked bow just above them. (Use hot glue to secure the tails and bow.)

12. Spread the bow loops, threading them into the flowers and herbs for a natural look. Knot sprigs of baby's breath into the ribbon tails if desired.

13. Store the completed bouquets between layers of white tissue paper in large covered boxes.

Bridesmaid's Bouquet

This bouquet includes more pink and appears brighter than the bride's bouquet because it was designed with gown colors in mind. Both the bride and her bridesmaid sister were small and dainty, so their bouquets were as well. At the bride's request, no ribbons were used on her sister's bouquet.

What You'll Need

Glue gun and glue sticks

Scissors

Project materials:

Floral picks

Purchased bouquet holder with Sahara foam

Purchased lace cuff for holder

Floral wire

White floral tape

Pink larkspur

White statice sinuata

Oregano blooms

Caspia

Lavender

Roses

Baby's breath

Sweet Annie artemisia

Pink statice sinuata

Anise hyssop

Time to Complete

About one and one-half hours

Method

Follow instructions for making the Bridal Bouquet (pages 86 to 87), but cut the flower and herb stems longer so that the finished nosegay will be wider.

Corsages

Making corsages isn't my favorite wedding task, but it's easier when I insist that the bride provide me with swatches of material from the dresses to be worn by the mother, mom-in-law, grandmoms, and other relatives. (I only ask for approximate color descriptions for the other participants' costumes.)

Don't forget to make corsages for yourself and your helper and to bring along at least one extra. I also bring extra pearly-topped corsage and boutonniere pins. These can be used in many ways during your decorating—even for pinning bows to reception table covers!

What You'll Need

(for one corsage)

Scissors	Cellophane bag
Wire cutters	Label
Glue gun and glue sticks	

Project materials:

Satin corsage leaves	Chenille stem
Ribbon	Floral wire
Green floral tape	Corsage pin

Flowers and greenery to match wearer's clothing:

Pink larkspur	White statice sinuata
Springerai fern	Roses
Baby's breath	

Time to Complete

If materials are nearby, about 20 to 30 minutes.

Method

1. Cut two sets of three satin corsage leaves each.

2. To form the base of the corsage, use floral tape to bind the stems of the leaves together in sets; then bind the two sets together as shown in the diagram.

3. Next, create two almost identical bouquets consisting of larkspur surrounded by fern and baby's breath, with a layer of statice sinuata on top.

4. Wire these bouquets on top of the leaf base, arranging the two sets of stems adjacent to one another and leaving an inch (2.5 cm) or less of the stems remaining uncovered in the center.

5. Hot-glue the roses in place.

6. Make a bow and attach it to the center of the corsage with half of a chenille stem.

7. Slip the completed corsage into a cellophane bag, fold the bag's open end over, and pin the bag closed with a corsage pin. Don't forget to label the bag with the future wearer's name.

8. Before presenting the corsage to its wearer, mist it lightly with water.

Boutonnieres

Remember the language of flowers? If not, turn to page 47. Well, along with the usual flowers that one expects to see in the groom's boutonniere, I include sprigs of thyme (courage), tarragon (lasting interest), and sage (wisdom). One bride begged me to include chamomile (patience), too!

Boutonnieres for men who will walk down the aisle with a bridal attendant are usually created to match the bouquet of the particular lady. Ushers' flowers, on the other hand, are all alike.

What You'll Need

(for one boutonniere)

Scissors

Cellophane bag

Labels

Project materials:

Satin corsage leaves

Green floral tape

Larkspur

Lavender

Springerai fern

White statice sinuata

Rose

Boutonniere pin

Time to Complete

About 20 minutes if materials are nearby

Method

1. Using satin corsage leaves as a backing, form a bunch of materials in your hand. In the project shown, I've used larkspur alongside lavender, surrounded by fern, with a top layer that contains statice on either side of a rose.

2. Use floral tape to attach the bunch to the corsage leaf stem.

3. To fill in the spaces between flowers, use floral tape to attach shorter pieces of fern to the front bottom surface.

4. Wrap any visible stem sections with floral tape.

5. Slip the boutonniere into a cellophane bag, fold the open end of the bag over, and secure the fold with the boutonniere pin. To make life easier at the ceremony, add a label with the wearer's name.

Floral Arrangement for Wedding Reception Table

Fresh from my herb gardens where they were gathered at dawn, these wonderful flowers rest in a silver bowl. (Decorate the table with draped tulle secured by large white satin bows embellished with ivy, hemlock, and the Crocheted Bells on page 93.) Of course, the table was later covered with silver trays bearing all sorts of delightful food, but a great deal of the conversation centered on the herbs and flowers. Naturally!

(continued on next page)

Flower Arrangement
for Wedding Reception Table (continued)

What You'll Need

Buckets of water

Shears

Scissors

Hammer to pound woody stems

Floral tape

Project materials:

Oasis floral foam	Lavender
Silver bowl	Soapwort
Mountain mint	Yarrow
Sweet Annie artemisia	Chicory
Silver king artemisia	Larkspur
Caspia	Statice sinuata
Baby's breath	Monarda
Cleome	Salvia victoria
Queen Anne's lace	Purple coneflowers
Roses	Southernwood
Phlox	Russian sage
Oregano	

Time to Complete

About 45 minutes, but only when all materials are within steps of your work table

Method

1. Place the oasis foam in the bowl, cover it with water, and allow it to sit for ten or fifteen minutes while it absorbs the water.

2. Insert the mint and artemisia to establish the height of the arrangement and to separate color areas.

3. Add the caspia and baby's breath.

4. Insert the large, colorful bloom heads.

5. Fill in spaces with the remaining flowers, but, for a natural garden feeling, work to keep the design free and light, not tight and rigid.

Crocheted Bells and Hearts

As a token of love, a relative of the bride had crocheted and starched these decorative wedding bells and hearts, which I was instructed to incorporate into the wedding decorations. A filament loop hanger was already in place on each piece.

After I'd embellished them, I tied the bells into the garland over the entrance to the chapel (page 79), under the tulle bow on the garland at the guest registry table (page 80), into the pew markers (page 83), and into bows on the reception tables. The hearts were placed in the midst of the ivy that encircled the wedding cake (page 77) and on reception tables.

What You'll Need

(to decorate one piece)

Glue gun and glue

Project materials:

Crocheted and starched wedding bell or heart

2 mountain mint leaves

1 sprig baby's breath

1 lavender bloom stalk

1 white globe amaranth

1 rose

Time to Complete

Five to ten minutes

Method

Using a glue gun (and the photos as guides), attach the herbs and flowers in the order listed.

I created this last-minute garland for the guest register (page 80) while I sat outdoors on the church steps. In my hand, you can see one of the small bouquets that I made and then wired to the rope. Many years ago, I discovered that a large basket is a handy way to carry wedding tools and ribbons to church. I was certainly glad I'd brought my trusty tools with me this time, as I'd never have been able to make this garland without my wire cutters and heavy-duty scissors.

Herbal Candle Ring

Wreaths such as this one served as centerpiece decorations at reception tables and as gifts to the ladies who assisted in serving the reception. Each ring was topped with a little bird to represent happiness. The bride purchased the ivory candles long before the wedding and brought them to my shop so that I could create wreaths perfectly sized to enhance them.

What You'll Need

    Glue gun and glue sticks
    Scissors

Project materials:

    10" (25.4 cm) floral foam wreath base
    Spanish moss
    Floral picks and pins
    Bird
    4" to 6" (10.2 to 15.2 cm) sprigs of:

        Sweet Annie artemisia
        Caspia
        White statice sinuata
        Pink statice sinuata
        White larkspur
        Pink larkspur
        Oregano blooms
        Lavender
        Pearly everlasting
        Silver king artemisia
        Roses

Time to Complete

Approximately one hour

Method

1. Cover the front surface and the inner and outer rims of the base with Spanish moss, using floral pins to hold it in place.

2. Attach picks to several bunches of sweet Annie and pick the bunches in place around the inner and outer rims of the wreath base. Keep the bunches on the inner rim short enough to leave space for the candle.

3. Fill in the front surface of the wreath with the remaining herbs and flowers, alternating caspia with colored herbs and saving the roses for last.

4. Hot-glue the bird in place.

5. Spray the completed wreath with a fixative; then place it in a covered box until you reach the church.

Decorations for Toasting Glasses

"May you have a long and happy life"—a proper toast for a young couple just starting out together! I attach small herbal bouquets to the stems of glasses used to propose this toast and to the cake knife and cake-serving silver pieces as well. Incidentally, do remember to find out whether the bride and groom are right- or left-handed so that your decorations will show up when the happy couple faces the camera.

What You'll Need

(for one decoration)

Scissors

Project materials:

Floral tape	Baby's breath
Floral wire	Oregano blooms
Springerai ferns	White satin ribbon
Pink larkspur	Chenille stem, cut in half
Lavender	

Time to Complete

About ten minutes

Method

1. In one hand, gather a small bouquet of ferns topped with larkspur, lavender, and baby's breath. Top with oregano blooms.

2. Wrap the bunched stems with floral tape.

3. Make a small satin-ribbon bow and wire its center to secure it.

4. Wrap the chenille stem around the wired bow, twisting it so that it will be ready to apply to a glass stem or silver handle at the reception.

5. Store the decoration in a tissue-filled box with lid.

6. At the reception site, attach the decoration by twisting the chenille stem around the stem of the glass and tucking its ends under the greenery.

Spiral Birch Wreath

With the light streaming through the beveled and frosted glass of this door, the spiral wreath seems to be frozen in space.

What You'll Need

Glue gun and glue sticks

Scissors

Project materials:

25" (63.5 cm) swirled birch wreath base

Caspia

Sheet moss

Yarrow

Globe amaranth

Roses

Crested celosia

Hydrangeas

Time to Complete

About two hours

Method

1. Cut the bloom ends of the caspia to about 5" to 7" (12.7 to 17.8 cm) long. Hot-glue them in place around the outer rim of the wreath base, among the birch branch swirls.

2. To hide the front surface of the base, hot-glue pieces of sheet moss around it.

3. Randomly hot-glue the other herbs around the sheet moss, applying them in the following order: yarrow, globe amaranth, roses, crested celosia, and hydrangeas. To ensure a light, airy look and feel, leave some space between the flowers and let the moss show through.

4. Spray the completed wreath with a fixative.

Garlic Braid

These 24 garlic bulbs are braided in sets of three, tied together, and decorated with oregano, bay leaves, and quince slices for your kitchen pleasure. Yes, you can break off the garlic and cook it, but only if you can bear to dismantle this decorative treasure.

(continued on next page)

Garlic Braid (continued)

What You'll Need

Glue gun and glue sticks

Project materials:

24 garlic bulbs with stems

Bay leaves

Oregano

Quince slices (purchased)

Raffia bow

Time to Complete

About an hour

Method

1. Braid the garlic in sets of three.

2. Tie all the braided bundles together with raffia 7" (17.8 cm) from the top and again just above the cluster of bulbs at the bottom.

3. Tie raffia around the braids 6" (15.2 cm) from the top, and form a loop to serve as a hanger.

4. As a background for the design, hot-glue several bay leaves along the stems.

5. Also hot-glue four quince slices along the stems, placing the largest at the base of the leaf background.

6. Hot-glue half of a quince slice at the top to make an uneven number and to carry the eye up the stems to the top of the design.

7. To soften the design, fill in between the garlic and quince slices with stems of oregano.

8. Tie on the raffia bow as shown in the photo.

9. If you plan to cook with the garlic, don't spray this project with a fixative!

Kitchen Garland

In a tiny cottage, simple embellishments are best, and what could be better than this fragrant garland, which combines the aromas of cinnamon sticks, bay leaves, nutmeg, and potpourri-filled cloth hearts? To make the fabric hearts, follow the basic sewing instructions on page 72.

What You'll Need

Electric drill with small bit

Wire cutters

Project materials:

3 fabric hearts filled with Citrus & Spice potpourri (page 67)

1" by 12" (2.5 by 30.5 cm) rag strips for two bows

Plastic-coated spool wire (20-gauge)

Whole bay leaves

Whole nutmegs

3" (7.6 cm) cinnamon sticks

Freeze-dried pomegranates

Time to Complete

Several hours. I usually assemble all the materials on a card table and string this garland at night while watching an old movie.

Method

1. Drill tiny holes through the pomegranates, cinnamon sticks, and nutmegs.

2. Cut a point at the free end of the spool wire so that you can use the wire itself as a needle. Leave the wire rolled on the spool. Although this garland is usually about 54" (137.2 cm) long, there's no way to tell exactly how much wire you'll need.

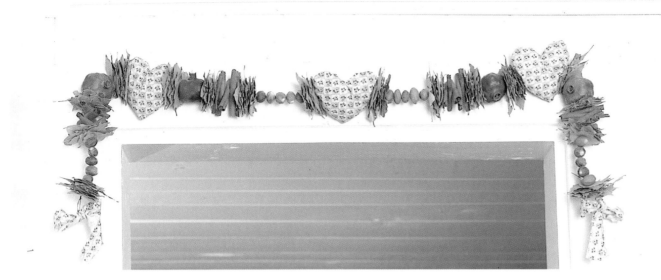

3. String the materials onto the wire in the order that follows, recutting the point of the wire as often as necessary:

    20 bay leaves

    5 nutmegs

    20 bay leaves

    5 cinnamon sticks

    20 bay leaves

    Pomegranate

    20 bay leaves

    Potpourri heart

    20 bay leaves

    Pomegranate

    20 bay leaves

    5 cinnamon sticks

    20 bay leaves

    5 nutmegs

    20 bay leaves

    Potpourri heart

    20 bay leaves

    5 nutmegs

    20 bay leaves

    5 cinnamon sticks

    20 bay leaves

    Pomegranate

    20 bay leaves

    Potpourri heart

    20 bay leaves

    Pomegranate

    20 bay leaves

    5 cinnamon sticks

    20 bay leaves

    5 nutmegs

    20 bay leaves

4. Roll enough wire from the spool to enable you to make a 1" (2.5 cm) loop at each end. Cut the wire and twist the ends to make these loops.

5. Push a rag strip through the wire loop at each end of the garland, and tie it into a bow. Cut the ends of the bow streamers on a diagonal.

Display this fragrant garland over a kitchen door, window, or cabinet.

Two-Tone Beauty

This one looks like an explosion in two colors! The red of the roses and feathered celosia contrasts nicely with the gray-white of the artemisia and caspia.

What You'll Need

    Glue gun and glue sticks

    Scissors

    Tweezers

Project materials:

    11" (27.9 cm) grapevine wreath base

    Floral tape

    Brown yarn

    Powis castle artemisia

    Caspia

    Feathered celosia

    Roses

Time to Complete

About an hour

Method

1. Form bunches, each about 6" (15.2 cm) long, of artemisia, caspia, and celosia, layered one on top of the other. Use green floral tape to wrap the stem ends of each bunch. (The stems of both caspia and celosia can scratch your skin.)

2. Use brown yarn to tie the bunches, one at a time, onto the grapevine wreath base, making sure to disguise the stem ends by overlapping the bunches. Cover the entire base.

3. Hot-glue the roses into the design adjacent to the celosia.

Wall Hanging

Glorious colors and random placement of a myriad of materials create the look of a summer garden on this piece.

What You'll Need

Glue gun and glue sticks

Scissors

Project materials:

9" by 12" (22.9 by 30.5 cm)) vine wall piece with arched back and 2"-tall (5.1 cm) "box" at base

Sheet moss

3" (7.6 cm) bird

Baby's breath

Yarrow

Lamb's ears

Roses

Hops

Pink globe amaranth

Sweet Annie artemisia

Crested celosia

Pansies (dried in an encyclopedia between facial tissues)

Oregano

Lavender

Time to Complete

One and one-half to two hours

Method

1. Roll sheet moss to fill the "box," and glue it in place.

2. Hot-glue the bird to the cross piece, as shown in the photo.

3. Hot-glue all the flower stems into place, aiming them at an invisible spot a little to the right of the box's center. Work from the back towards the front, balancing the textures, stem lengths, and colors. The large yarrow bloom, right over the spot, will be the last piece you glue into the design. Remember to keep the materials far enough apart to create the light and airy appearance of a real garden.

Wild Thing

An unusual color combination and a wildly free twig base set this dramatic wreath apart.
The twig branches jut out from the base in three directions to make a full visual impact.

What You'll Need

> Glue gun and glue sticks
>
> Scissors

Project materials:

> 24" (61.0 cm) twig base
>
> White larkspur
>
> Caspia
>
> Poppy pod heads, dyed pale gray-blue
>
> Wheat seed heads
>
> Lavender blooms
>
> Bittersweet
>
> Lions' ears
>
> Oregano blooms
>
> Yarrow bloom heads
>
> Chinese lantern pods

Time to Complete

About one and one-half to two hours

Method

1. Cut the stems of each material to the same length, ranging from 4" to 8" (10.2 to 20.3 cm) for the various herbs and flowers. This range will add depth to your design.

2. Hot-glue the white larkspur stems around the wreath base, spacing them at equal distances.

3. Hot-glue the caspia into place in a similar fashion.

4. Hot-glue the remaining dried materials, keeping colors, textures, and forms balanced around the wreath.

5. Spray the completed wreath with a fixative.

Bay Leaf Topiary

Encourage your customers to use this charming topiary as an accent near a table lamp or to buy two and place them on either side of a mantel. The soft green of the bay leaves provides a soothing effect that won't compete visually with other decorative objects in the same vicinity.

What You'll Need

Glue gun and glue sticks

Sharp knife

Project materials:

Two 3" (7.6 cm) rigid polystyrene balls

2-1/2" to 3-1/2" (6.8 to 8.9 cm) clay pot

1/2" by 7-1/2" (1.3 by 19.1 cm) wood dowel

Straight pins

Raffia

Sheet moss

Bay leaves

Rose

Time to Complete

Approximately one hour

Method

1. Hot-glue one of the foam balls into the clay pot to serve as a base. If it's too large, just use a sharp knife to pare it down to size.

2. Make a trunk for the topiary by inserting the dowel into the center of the ball.

3. Apply hot glue to the top of the dowel and push the dowel into the top of the second ball. Make sure that the dowel stands straight and that the upper ball is centered over the lower.

4. Disguise the visible surface of the lower ball by hot-gluing sheet moss around it.

5. Using straight pins and starting at the top, cover the upper ball with bay leaves.

6. When the ball is completely hidden, hot-glue the raised ends of the outermost leaves to hold them down. As you do this, remove the straight pins, continuing until all pins have been removed and all the leaves are firmly affixed.

7. Make a raffia bow and tie it in place with a knot, as shown in the photo.

8. Hot-glue a dried rose on top of the knot in the bow.

River Valley Bed and Breakfast Wreath

River Valley Bed and Breakfast is located in Watauga County, North Carolina, and was once the home of one of the first physicians in this section of the mountains. The innkeeper, Kerry, has lovingly restored and decorated her home, combining history and comfort to make her guests feel welcome. The colors of this large, custom-designed wreath repeat shades in the dining-room carpet, the wallpaper, and the china.

What You'll Need

Glue gun and glue sticks

Project materials:

18" (45.7 cm) straw wreath base

Tulle

Chenille stems

Floral picks and pins

Silver king artemisia

Mountain mint

Wheat

Yarrow

Anise hyssop

Lepidium (dyed blue to pick up wallpaper color)

Pearly everlasting

Crested celosia

Hydrangeas

Roses

Time to Complete

About four hours

Method

1. Wrap the wreath base in tulle (see page 54).

2. Use the chenille stem to make a looped hanger at the top of the wreath.

3. Attach ten bunches of silver king artemisia, approximately 6" to 8" (15.2 to 20.3 cm) long and 4" to 6" (10.2 to 15.2 cm) wide to floral picks. Insert the picked bunches around the inner rim of the wreath base.

4. Repeat Step 3 around the outer rim, using 25 to 27 bunches or more; your goal is to create a full feathery effect.

5. Around the outer rim of the wreath base, just on top of the artemisia, pick in about 20 bunches of mountain mint, each 5" to 7" (12.7 to 17.8 cm) long and 4" to 6" (10.2 to 15.2 cm) across the top. The number will be determined by the size of your dried mint leaves.

6. Make eight wheat bouquets, each 4" to 6" long, with three stalks of wheat apiece. Use floral pins to attach these over the mountain mint, spacing them evenly.

7. Attach eight large yarrow heads to floral picks and insert them adjacent to the wheat bouquets.

8. Next to the yarrow, pick in eight bunches of anise hyssop. Each bunch should contain three to five blooms and be 5" to 7" long.

9. In the remaining uncovered spaces, use floral picks and your glue gun to weave a tapestry of eight lepidium, fourteen pearly everlastings, eleven crested celosia, and twenty-six hydrangea heads. The size of each material will determine the exact numbers needed here. Although most of these items can be picked, hydrangeas will need the added security of some hot glue to stay in place.

10. Last but not least come the roses. Pick four of them into the wreath, scattering them evenly throughout the design.

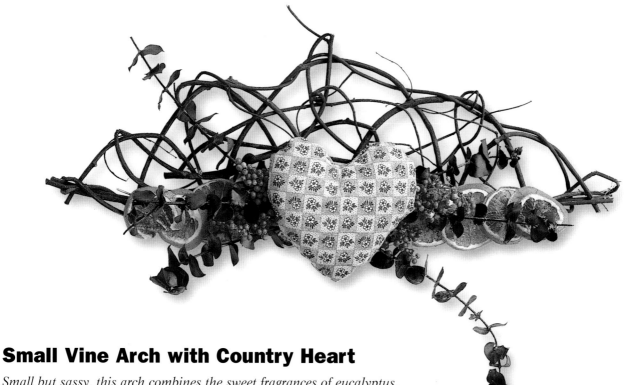

Small Vine Arch with Country Heart

Small but sassy, this arch combines the sweet fragrances of eucalyptus, orange, and potpourri (inside the heart sachet). Pepper berries from Florida serve as accents to brighten the design.

What You'll Need

Glue gun and glue sticks

Scissors

Project materials:

Purchased 15" (38.1 cm) vine arch

Brown yarn

Eucalyptus stems

Dried orange slices

Pepper berries

Potpourri-filled sachet heart, 4" by 4"
(10.2 by 10.2 cm)

Time to Complete

After heart is made and filled, about 15 minutes

Method

1. To make the fabric heart, use the basic sewing instructions on page 72.

2. Using the photo as a guide, hot-glue the oranges onto the arch, overlapping them slightly. (Remember to leave room for the heart.)

3. Gather three stems of eucalyptus topped with two sprigs of pepper berries and tie the bunch over the orange slices on the left side of center.

4. Repeat to tie eucalyptus and berries on the right side.

5. Hot-glue the potpourri heart in place at the center of the base, over the yarn and stem ends.

6. Spray the completed project with a fixative.

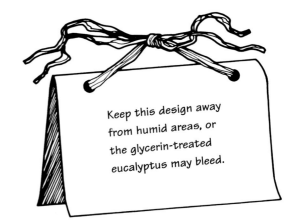

Keep this design away from humid areas, or the glycerin-treated eucalyptus may bleed.

Blended Perfection

Its soft grays, greens, and pinks will soothe and delight the viewer, but the true perfection of this wreath comes with the blended fragrance of its mingled herbal aromas. Gorgeous!

What You'll Need

    Glue gun and glue sticks

    Scissors

Project materials:

    18" (45.7 cm) straw wreath base

    Tulle

    Chenille stem

    Floral picks and pins

    Silver king artemisia

    Mountain mint sprigs

    Thyme blossoms

    Crested celosia heads

    Strawflowers

    Lavender blooms

    Pearly everlasting

    Hydrangea blossoms

Time to Complete

About three hours

Method

1. Mist all materials with water for easier handling.

2. Wrap the straw wreath base in tulle (see page 54).

3. Make a hanger by twisting a chenille stem around the wreath base.

4. Form 12 bunches of artemisia, each 5" to 6" (12.7 to 15.2 cm) long and 4" to 6" (10.2 to 15.2 cm) wide and attach a floral pick to each one. Insert these around the inner rim of the wreath base, with the top of each bunch hiding the bottom of the preceding bunch. All the bunches should "move" in the same direction.

5. Make 28 more bunches of artemisia, each 7" (17.8 cm) long and 4" (10.2 cm) wide at the blossom end. Add picks and attach to the outer rim of the wreath base.

6. Make three- to five-stem bunches of mountain mint, 5" to 7" long (12.7 to 17.8 cm). Then, working from the outer rim towards the front surface, use floral pins to attach the bunches to the base, layering the stems as you do.

7. Using floral pins, attach five groups of herbs around the top surface of the wreath, between the artemisia on the outer rim and the mountain mint. In each of the five groups, include a large head of crested celosia, a bunch of thyme, a large bunch of strawflowers, and a large bunch of lavender, evenly spacing them all.

8. In the remaining spaces between the herbs and the artemisia, use floral pins to insert bunches of pearly everlasting and hydrangea. The latter will adhere best with a little help from your hot-glue gun.

9. Finish off with a fixative spray.

Wall Basket

This design, built upon a flat basket, will grace a covered porch, where first impressions are so important, or a wall or door.

What You'll Need

Glue gun and glue sticks

Scissors

Project materials:

13" by 18" (33.0 by 45.7 cm) flat wall basket (created by McFadden's Vines and Wreaths, Butler, Tennessee)

Rubber bands

Holly fern fronds, preserved

Hydrangea clusters

Yarrow blooms

Crested celosia heads

Larkspur bloom heads

Caspia blooms

Mint bloom heads

Globe amaranth

Anise hyssop

Baby's breath

Strawflowers

Bow (optional)

Time to Complete

A little more than an hour

Method

1. Hot-glue a couple of holly fern fronds in a diagonal line across the basket, with their tips pointing away from it.

2. Hot-glue hydrangeas across the holly, placing the smallest bloom clusters at each end.

3. Make several bunches of globe amaranth, securing the stems in each bunch with a tightly twisted rubber band.

4. Work the herbs into the design, gluing them in place in the following order and using the photo as a placement guide: yarrow, celosia, larkspur, caspia, mint blooms, globe amaranth bunches, anise hyssop, baby's breath, and strawflowers.

5. Spray the completed project with a fixative.

6. For a special touch, add a large bow to the left side of the design, under the floral band where the handle meets the basket.

Small Spiral Wreath

A very talented lady, Betty McFadden (McFadden's Vines and Wreaths, Butler, Tennessee), created the swirled birch base for this project. An overlay of plumosa fern topped with dried herbs, everlastings, and sunflowers makes for a delightful wreath.

What You'll Need

Glue gun and glue sticks

Scissors

Project materials:

7" (17.8 cm) swirled birch wreath base

Plumosa fern

3 dried sunflowers

Statice sinuata

German statice

Strawflowers

Yarrow

Globe amaranth

Pearly everlasting

Rudbeckia

Roses

Two birds and ribbon (optional)

Time to Complete

About one hour

Method

1. Hot-glue the plumosa fern around the outer and inner rims of the wreath base, making sure that it all points in the same direction.

2. To divide the base into three equal sections, hot-glue three sunflowers to the front surface.

3. Hot-glue 2" to 2-1/2" (5.1 to 6.4 cm) pieces of purple statice sinuata blooms around the front surface.

4. Hot-glue several sprigs of white German statice along the inner and outer rims of the base. These will separate and lighten the colors.

5. Hot-glue the strawflowers and yarrow heads into place.

6. Glue the pink globe amaranth heads into the design, varying their sizes for interest.

7. Fill in the design with pearly everlasting heads, rudbeckia, and roses. Strive to balance colors.

8. Spray the completed wreath with a fixative to preserve and protect it.

9. Although this wreath lacks them, a couple of little birds would fit nicely into its design. Position the birds so that they face one another across the wreath and glue a ribbon between their beaks.

Warm Weather Wonder

*This colorful wreath is fashioned around a dramatic spiral birch base.
Its colors are reminiscent of a summer garden and beg to brighten
a home interior on a dreary day.*

What You'll Need

Glue gun and glue sticks

Scissors

Tweezers

Project materials:

24" (61.0 cm) birch wreath base with swirled sides

Brown yarn

Mountain mint

German statice

Anise hyssop blooms

Yarrow

Globe thistle

Dried fern

Crested celosia

Roses

Heather

Poppy pods

Globe amaranth

Lavender

Tansy

Rudbeckia

Daisies

Statice sinuata

Time to Complete

About two hours if materials are assembled in advance

Method

1. Layer 6" to 8" (15.2 to 20.3 cm) lengths of mountain mint and German statice in your hand, and top the bunch with anise hyssop, yarrow, and globe thistle. Using brown yarn, tie the bunch onto the front surface of the wreath base. The easiest way to do this is to first use tweezers to thread the yarn into and out of the base, inserting it to about half the base's depth. Then, with the two loose ends, tie a double knot around the bunched herbs.

2. Repeat Step 1 until the wreath base is completely covered, making sure that each bunch of herbs covers the tied ends of the preceding bunch.

3. Hot-glue the other stems into the design in random locations, applying them in this order: fern, crested celosia, roses, heather, poppy pods, globe amaranth, lavender, tansy, rudbeckia, daisy, and statice sinuata. You'll find that the stem ends of herbs are easier to insert into the base if they're cut to points.

4. Spray the completed wreath with a fixative.

Refrigerator Magnet Wreath

For people who dare to say they don't have room for a wreath, here's one created specifically for a refrigerator door.

What You'll Need

Glue gun and glue sticks

Scissors

Project materials:

5" (12.7 cm) faux evergreen wreath

Three 3/4" (1.9 cm) button-type magnets

Yarrow

Bittersweet

Globe amaranth

German statice

Time to Complete

Fifteen to twenty minutes

Method

1. Break the yarrow heads into pieces about 1" (2.5 cm) wide; then hot-glue them around the wreath base, alternating placement on the inner and outer rims.

2. Hot-glue tiny sprigs of bittersweet around the front surface of the wreath.

3. Fill in the remaining spaces by hot-gluing globe amaranth heads into them.

4. Add some little wisps of German statice.

5. Turn the wreath over and hot-glue the magnets in place at the twelve o'clock, five o'clock, and eight o'clock positions.

Red & Green Eucalyptus Swag

Elegant eucalyptus offers its distinctive fragrance wherever it's displayed.
This swag design is simplified through the use of a metal framework designed by
A.F. Hillman's, Patterson, New Jersey. This straight wire piece with six evenly-
spaced sets of clamps along its length is especially useful for making swags.

What You'll Need

Scissors

Project materials:

18" (45.7 cm) metal framework

6 large bunches eucalyptus, mixed red and green, approximately 10" (25.4 cm) long with fan-shaped spread of 8" to 12" (20.3 to 30.5 cm)

Chenille stem

Floral wire

Wired ribbon for ten-loop bow

Time to Complete

About 25 minutes, including cutting and bow

Method

1. Spread the wire clamps into the open position.

2. Form several bouquets of mixed red and green eucalyptus. Starting at either end and remembering to balance shape, length, and size, place these against the metal framework and secure them by closing the clamps tightly. As you work towards the center, be sure to cover the stem ends of each bouquet with the leaf ends of the next.

3. Place the final two bouquets against the center of the framework, with their stem ends adjacent to each other. Clamp firmly.

4. Make a large bow with the wired ribbon, using floral wire to secure its center.

5. Use a chenille stem to make a hanging loop around the center of the design.

6. Tie the bow over the center of the design to hide the clamps.

7. Shape the bow as desired by bending the wired ribbon.

112 ✤

Oregano and Pearly Everlasting Wreath

Fresh from the gardens, this wreath is marvelously fragrant. A color scheme of soft gray-green, cream, and peachy pink makes it just right for a feminine accent.

What You'll Need

Glue gun and glue sticks

Scissors

Project materials:

20" by 14" (50.8 by 35.6 cm)
   oval grapevine wreath base

Brown yarn

Pearly everlasting

Oregano blooms

Feathered celosia

Dried Sonia roses

Time to Complete

About 30 to 45 minutes

Method

1. Mist all materials with water.

2. Form nine bunches of pearly everlasting, each 6" by 6" (15.2 by 15.2 cm) and nine bunches of oregano blooms, also 6" by 6".

3. Cover the wreath base by tying the bunches onto the front surface with lengths of brown yarn, double-knotting and trimming the yarn. Alternate the pearly everlasting and oregano, placing the top of each bunch over the bottom of the previously applied bunch.

4. Using the photo as a color guide, hot-glue nine celosia heads evenly around the wreath's front surface.

5. Hot-glue the roses in place.

6. Spray the finished design with a fixative.

Tiny Birdbaths

Can you believe that these tiny birdbaths, made for the most part with scraps leftover from other projects, are only 4" (10.2 cm) tall? The little birds sitting on the rims add a touch of reality. Considering their dainty herbs and flowers, these miniatures pack quite a wallop visually.

What You'll Need

(for one birdbath)

Glue gun and glue sticks

Project materials:

Sheet moss

2" (5.1 cm) clay pot

3-1/2" (8.9 cm) clay saucer

Quick-drying adhesive

Scraps of colorful herbs and flowers:

Silver king artemisia or tarragon bloom stems

Tiny mountain mint leaves

Baby's breath

German statice

Assorted herb flowers (or bits of flowers)

Tiny rose buds

Mushroom bird

Spray fixative

Time to Complete

Not long! I usually complete Steps 1 and 2 and then forget about the project for a couple of weeks. When I'm ready to start again, I form my own assembly line to complete several birdbaths at one work session.

Method

1. Before starting this project, select a color scheme and choose flowers accordingly. To balance the colors in the design, use three or five blooms of each color selected.

2. Wipe clean the bases of your clay pot and saucer. Then glue them together with a quick-drying adhesive that is suitable for porous surfaces. Let stand until completely dry.

3. Turn the assembled pieces so that the pot is on the bottom. Hot-glue moss around the top rim of the saucer birdbath and at one spot on the base.

4. Hot-glue an artemisia stem into the moss on the base. Wind the top of the stem over the rim of the bird-bath, attaching it there with glue as well.

5. Hot-glue the mountain mint leaves around the moss at even intervals to form the background for flowers yet to come.

6. Hot-glue baby's breath, German statice, the herb flowers, and the roses throughout the leaves and moss, taking care to balance the colors.

7. Hot-glue the bird to the rim.

8. Spray the finished project with a fixative.

Carolyn's Wreath

This wreath was custom designed to pick up the colors of the great room in a mountain home. The chimney that serves as its background was made with stones gathered on the property where the house was subsequently built.
My plan was to create a beautiful wreath for a beautiful lady.

(continued on next page)

Carolyn's Wreath (continued)

What You'll Need

Scissors

Glue gun and glue sticks

Project materials:

26" (66.0 cm) straw wreath base

Tulle

Chenille stems

Floral picks and pins

Silver king artemisia	German statice
Thyme	Globe thistle
Anise hyssop	Larkspur
Globe amaranth	Lavender
Heather	Mexican sage
Hydrangeas	Mountain mint
Apple mint	Parsley
Basil	Pearly everlasting
Black peppermint	Roses
Celosia	Statice sinuata
German sage	Yarrow

Time to Complete

Most of one day

Method

1. Wrap the straw wreath base with tulle (see page 54).

2. Use chenille stems to form a hanging loop, doubling the stems to support the considerable weight of the wreath.

3. Create bunches of artemisia at least 6" long and add picks to them. Insert these around the inner rim of the wreath base.

4. Repeat to cover the outer rim of the wreath base.

5. Using the photo as a guide, pin staggered bunches of thyme along both the outer and inner rims.

6. Pick small bunches of anise hyssop into the design.

7. Add picked bunches of globe amaranth along the front surface.

8. Fill in the remaining spaces with the other herbs, alternating hydrangeas with more colorful flower heads. If you're short on flowers, use gray artemisia instead.

9. Spray the completed wreath with a fixative.

Tussie Mussie

In Elizabethan England, people carried tussie mussies—small nosegays made up of aromatic herbs and flowers—to help disguise the dreadful stench of London's streets. These serviceable bouquets often included herbs thought to be disinfectants (lavender, rosemary, and rue, for example) and protection from plague and other diseases. Traditionally, whether fresh or dried flowers were used, a rose was placed in the center. By Victorian times, tussie mussies had also become a favorite way to send messages to friends and lovers. Each herb and flower had its own accepted meaning (see page 47).

Tussie mussies may be small enough to use as ornaments on Christmas trees or large enough to serve as bridal bouquets, and their forms can vary to suit the creator. No matter what size they are, your customers will appreciate a customer instruction card that explains the history of tussie mussies and that provides the meaning of each herb or flower in the one they're buying.

What You'll Need

Scissors

Glue gun and glue sticks

Project materials:

6" (15.2 cm) paper doily cuff

Floral tape

Satin ribbon

Floral wire

Mountain mint leaves

Rose

Lavender

Pearly everlasting

Globe amaranth

Santolina

Oregano blooms

Time to Complete

If materials are handy, 20 to 30 minutes

Method

1. Use hot glue to attach a ring of mountain mint leaves around the inner cone of the paper cuff. Five or six leaves will usually do, depending on their sizes. Set aside.

2. Cut a 6" to 8" (15.2 to 20.3 cm) length of floral tape.

3. Cut the rose stem to 6" in length, and near the flower head, wrap the stem with one complete circle of floral tape. (Don't cut the tape from the roll yet.)

4. Around the wrapped stem, position three equally-spaced lavender bloom heads; then bring the roll of tape around once more to secure the three stems to the rose stem.

5. Continue to add flowers in sets of three, securing each set by bringing the roll of tape around them as you fill out the design from the central rose outward. Spiral the tape gradually down to the bottom of the rose stem as you go.

6. When the nosegay is wide enough to fill the doily cuff, cut the gathered stems to about 5" (12.7 cm) in length and retape the entire bundle from top to bottom.

7. Insert the nosegay into the cuff.

8. Tape the cuff securely onto the stems.

9. Make a ribbon bow, wire its center, and hot-glue it between the leaf ring and flowers.

Plumosa Wreath

Dainty and delicate looking, this wreath is a garden to hang for the sheer joy of colorful symmetry. Because there is very little fragrance in these herbs, the wreath should be displayed for its visual impact.

What You'll Need

Glue gun and glue sticks

Scissors

Project materials:

21" (53.3 cm) plumosa fern wreath base

Chenille stem

Hydrangea clusters (Holland dried and bleached)

Purple statice sinuata

White statice sinuata

Crested celosia

Baby's breath

Yarrow

Globe amaranth

Strawflowers

Sonia roses

Santolina blooms

Time to Complete

About one hour

Method

1. Make a hanger for the wreath by twisting one-half of a chenille stem around the wire frame of the base.

2. Before gluing any of your materials in place, use the photo as a guide to arrange the flowers around the wreath base, balancing colors, shapes, and forms for a pleasing design. Do place the santolina blooms next to the roses, as their yellow color will draw the eye towards the latter.

3. In the order listed, hot-glue the materials in place, being careful to hide stems under ferns and other materials.

Be sure to keep this wreath away from direct sunlight.

Sweet Annie and Oregano Wreath

Rose hues and fragrant herbs promise a stunning display and sweet scents wherever this wreath is displayed. If you hang it in the bathroom or kitchen, steam will activate its fragrance and sweeten the air in the surrounding space.

What You'll Need

Scissors

Glue gun and glue sticks

Project materials:

9" (22.9 cm) straw wreath base

Tulle

Chenille stem

Floral pins

Sweet Annie artemisia

Oregano blooms

Baby's breath

Lavender

Sarracenia lily

Crested celosia

Roses

Lunaria

Time to Complete

If all materials are assembled in advance, about one and one-half to two hours.

Method

1. Wrap the straw wreath base with tulle (see page 54).

2. Make a wreath hanger by wrapping a chenille stem around the base.

3. Cover the outer rim of the wreath with about fifteen bunches of sweet Annie, each approximately 7" (17.8 cm) long; use floral pins to attach them.

4. Cover the inner rim of the wreath with bunches of oregano, attaching them with floral pins as well.

5. Just inside the oregano, add another layer of herbs, alternating bunches of sweet Annie and oregano blooms.

6. Fill the front surface of the wreath with alternating clusters of baby's breath, lavender, Sarracenia lily, celosia, and sweet Annie.

7. Hot-glue the roses and lunaria into the design.

Vine Arch with Lamb's Ears

This vine arch is decorated with soft colors and could be displayed over a bed, above a door, or even on a covered porch. Purchase the arch in a craft store; decorating it won't take long at all.

What You'll Need

Glue gun and glue sticks

Scissors

Project materials:

Purchased 19" (48.3 cm) vine arch

Brown yarn

Rubber bands

Lamb's ear stems

Lavender bunches

Oregano bloom stems

7" (17.8 cm) raffia bow

Dried pomegranates

Dried orange slices

Time to Complete

About 20 minutes

Method

1. Form two bunches of lamb's ear stems, 10" to 11" (25.4 to 27.9 cm) long, with three stems per bunch. Hold each bunch together loosely with a rubber band.

2. On top of each bunch, rest several 8" to 9" (20.3 to 22.9 cm) stems of lavender, slipping these into the rubber bands as well.

3. Lay three stems of oregano blooms, 6" to 7" (15.2 to 17.8 cm) long atop the lavender, slipping these into the rubber band to achieve a layered look of gray, lavender, and rosy pink.

4. Position the two completed nosegays at the center of the arch base, with their stems overlapping. Tie them securely to the base with brown yarn, and trim the yarn close to the double knot that you tie.

5. Use yarn to tie a raffia bow in place over the bunches.

6. Hot-glue three pomegranates and three orange slices under and on top of the raffia bow to hide the knotted yarn.

7. Spray the completed project with a fixative.

Pussy Willow Wreath

The spectacular presentation of this wreath is the result of its wild swirl of pussy willow stems. Use only 12"- to 15"-long (30.5 to 38.1 cm) stem tips. I cut mine along the creek bank during the coldest month of the year. Gardening customers seem to be fond of the little clay pots that are tucked into the raffia bow.

What You'll Need

Glue gun and glue sticks

Project materials:

24" (61.0 cm) grapevine wreath base

Floral picks and pins

3 chenille stems

3 tiny clay pots

Raffia bow

Dried pussy willow stems

German statice

Strawflowers

Purple coneflowers

Yarrow

Mexican bush sage

Soapwort

Crested celosia

Anise hyssop

Spanish moss

Time to Complete

About three hours

Method

1. Sort the pussy willow stems into sets of two and attach a floral pick to each set. Then hot-glue the sets around the outer rim of the wreath base, spacing them evenly and placing each set at an angle.

2. To accent the colors you'll add later, create a light background by hot-gluing the German statice among the pussy willow stems, around both rims and the front surface of the wreath base.

3. In the order given, hot-glue the strawflowers, purple coneflowers, yarrow, Mexican bush sage, soapwort, and crested celosia around the front surface.

4. Hot-glue the anise hyssop at even intervals throughout the design.

5. To disguise the wreath form underneath, hot-glue small wads of Spanish moss around the inner rim.

6. To attach each clay pot, first fold a chenille stem in half and push the folded end down through the hole in the bottom of the pot so that the fold protrudes through to the outside. Slip a floral pin through the loop and twist the loose ends of the chenille stem into a knot inside the pot. Hot-glue sheet moss over the knot to hide it; then hot-glue a rose onto the moss. To incorporate the pot into the design, press the floral pin into the wreath base and glue into place.

7. Hot-glue a raffia bow between the three pots on the base.

8. Spray the completed wreath with a fixative.

Common and Latin Names

ALLSPICE	*Pimenta dioica*
ANGELICA	*Angelica archangelica*
ANISE HYSSOP	*Agastache foeniculum*
ANISE (SEEDS)	*Pimpinella anisum*
ANISE, STAR	*Illicium verum*
APPLE	*Malus spp.*
ARBORVITAE	*Thuja occidentalis*
ARTEMISIA	*Artemisia ludoviciana var. silver king, silver queen, and Powis castle*
BABY'S BREATH	*Gypsophila paniculata*
BASIL	*Ocimum basilicum*
BAY	*Laurus nobilis*
BEE BALM	*Monarda didyma*
BELL PEPPER	*Capsicum*
BITTERSWEET	*Celastrus*
BLACK PEPPER	*Piper nigrum*
BLACK-EYED SUSAN	*Rudbeckia hirta*
BORAGE	*Borage officinalis*
BOXWOOD	*Buxus*
BUGLEWEED	*Ajuga reptans*
BUTTERFLY BUSH	*Buddleia davidii*
CALENDULA, POT MARIGOLD	*Calendula officinalis*
CANDYTUFT	*Iberis sempervirens*
CARDAMOM	*Elettaria cardamomum*
CASPIA	*Limonium bellidifolium*
CATNIP	*Nepeta cataria*
CELERY	*Apium graveolens*
CELOSIA, CRESTED (COCKSCOMB)	*Celosia cristata*
CELOSIA, FEATHERED	*Celosia plumosa*
CHAMOMILE	*Anthemis nobilis*
CHERVIL	*Anthriscus cerefolium*
CHICORY	*Chichorium intybus*
CHINESE LANTERN	*Physalis alkekengi*
CHIVE	*Allium schoenoprasum*
CHRYSANTHEMUM	*Chrysanthemum*
CINNAMON	*Cinnamomum zeylanicum*
CLEOME	*Cleome spinosa*
CLOVE	*Syzygium aromaticum*
COLUMBINE	*Aquilegia*
COMFREY	*Symphytum officinale*

COREOPSIS	*Coreopsis*
COSMOS	*Cosmos*
DAISY	*Cosmos Bipinnatus*
DAISY FLEABANE	*Erigeron annuus*
DAYLILY	*Hemerocallis*
DELPHINIUM	*Delphinium ajacis*
EUCALYPTUS	*Eucalyptus*
FENNEL	*Foeniculum vulgare*
FERN, SPRINGERAI	*Asparagus densifloras*
FERN, PLUMOSA	*Asparagus setaceus*
FERN, HOLLY	*Cyrtomium falcatum*
FEVERFEW	*Chrysanthemum parthenium*
FOXGLOVE	*Digitalis purpurea*
FRENCH TARRAGON	*Artemisia dracunculus*
GARLIC	*Allium sativum*
GERANIUM, ROSE	*Pelargonium graveolens*
GERMANDER	*Teucrium chamaedrys*
GLOBE AMARANTH	*Gomphrena globosa*
GLOBE THISTLE	*Echinops ritro*
GOLDENROD	*Solidago*
GRAPEFRUIT	*Citrus paradisi*
HEATHER	*Calluna vulgaris*
HEMLOCK	*Tsuga canadensis*
HIBISCUS	*Hibiscus sabdariffa*
HOLLYHOCK	*Alcea rosea*
HONEYSUCKLE	*Lonicera caprifolium*
HOPS	*Humulus lupulus*
HYDRANGEA	*Hydrangea paniculata grandiflora*
HYSSOP	*Hyssopus officinalis*
IRIS, DUTCH	*Iris Xiphium*
IRIS, SIBERIAN	*Iris Sibirica*
IVY	*Hedera*
JEWELWEED	*Impatiens capensis*
JOE-PYE WEED	*Eupatorium purpureum*
LAMB'S EARS	*Stachys officinalis*
LANTANA	*Lantana camdra*
LARKSPUR	*Delphinium hybridum*
LAVENDER	*Lavandula angustifolia, munstead, vera, stoechas, hidcote, nana, lanata*

LEMON	*Citrus limon*	RUE	*Ruta graveolens*
LEMON BALM	*Melissa officinalis*	RUSSIAN OLIVE	*Elaeagnus angustifolia*
LEMON GRASS	*Cymbopogon citratum*	RUSSIAN SAGE	*Perovskia atriplicifolia*
LEMON VERBENA	*Aloysia triphylla*	SAGE	*Salvia officinalis*
LEPIDIUM	*Lepidium*	SAGE, MEXICAN BUSH	*Salvia Mexicana*
LILAC	*Syringa vulgaris*	SAGE, PINEAPPLE	*Salvia rutilans*
LILY, BLACKBERRY	*Belamcanda chinensis*	SALAD BURNET	*Poterium sanguisorba*
LILY, MADONNA	*Lilium candidum*	SANDALWOOD	*Pterocarpus santalinus*
LION'S-EAR	*Leonotis nepetifolia*	SANTOLINA	*Chamaecyparissus virens*
LOBELIA	*Lobelia inflata*	SARRACENIA LILY	*Lillium*
MARJORAM	*Origanum majorana*	SASSAFRAS	*Sassafras albidium*
MINT	*Mentha*	SAVORY	*Satureja hortensis*
MINT, APPLE	*Mentha suaveolens*	SESAME	*Sesamum indicum*
MINT, MOUNTAIN	*Pycnanthemum*	SHASTA DAISY	*Leucanthemum superbum*
MONEY PLANT	*Lunaria*	SNOW-IN-SUMMER	*Cerastium tomentosum*
MUGWORT	*Artemisia lactiflora*	SOAPWORT	*Saponaria officinalis*
NASTURTIUM	*Tropaeolum majus*	SOUTHERWOOD	*Artemisia abrotanum*
NIGELLA, LOVE-IN-A-MIST	*Nigella damascena*	SPANISH MOSS	*Tillandsia usneoides*
NUTMEG	*Myristica fragrans*	SPEARMINT	*Mentha spicata*
ONION	*Allium*	STATICE, ANNUAL	*Statice sinuata*
ORANGE	*Citrus sinensis*	STATICE, GERMAN	*Limonium tatarica*
OREGANO	*Origanum onites*	STRAWFLOWER	*Helichrysum bracteatum*
ORRIS	*Iris germanica var. florentina*	SUNFLOWER	*Helianthus*
PANSY	*Viola*	SWEET ALYSSUM	*Alyssum maritimum*
PARSLEY	*Petroselinum crispum*	SWEET ANNIE	*Artemisia annua*
PEARLY EVERLASTING	*Anaphalis margaritacea*	SWEET PEA	*Lathyrus odoratus*
PENNYROYAL	*Mentha pulegium*	TANSY	*Tanacetum vulgare*
PEONY	*Paeonia officinalis*	TANSY, FERN LEAF	*Tanacetum v. crispum*
PEPPERMINT, BLACK	*M. xp. crispa*	TARRAGON	*Artemisia dranunculus*
PEPPERMINT, CURLY	*M. piperita*	THYME	*Thymus vulgaris*
PHLOX	*Phlox drummondii*	TILIA	*Ternstroemia*
PINKS	*Dianthus*	TURTLEHEAD	*Chelone lionii*
POMEGRANATE	*Punica granatum*	VANILLA	*Vanilla planifolia*
POPPY	*Papaver rhoeas*	WATER HYACINTH	*Eichhornia crassipes*
PURPLE CONEFLOWER	*Echinacea purpurea*	WHEAT	*Triticum*
QUEEN ANNE'S LACE	*Daucus carota*	WINGED EVERLASTINGS	*Ammobium*
QUINCE	*Cydonia*	WORMWOOD	*Artemisia absinthium*
RASPBERRY	*Rubus idaeus*	YARROW	*Achillea millefolium*
ROSE	*Rosa*	ZINNIA	*Zinnia elegans*
ROSEMARY	*Rosmarinum officinalis*		

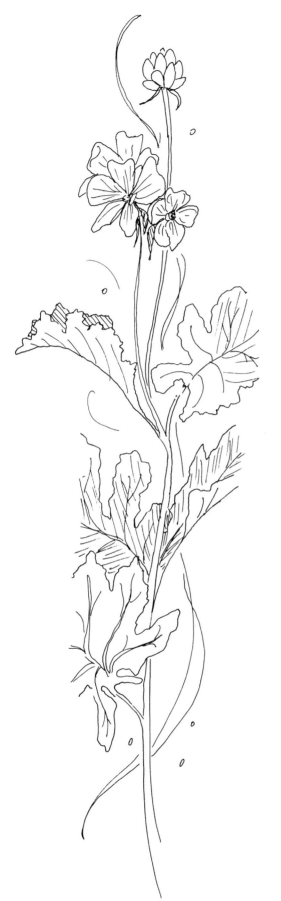

Metric Conversions

Lengths

Inches	CM	Inches	CM
1/8	0.3	20	50.8
1/4	0.6	21	53.3
3/8	1.0	22	55.9
1/2	1.3	23	58.4
5/8	1.6	24	61.0
3/4	1.9	25	63.5
7/8	2.2	26	66.0
1	2.5	27	68.6
1-1/4	3.2	28	71.1
1-1/2	3.8	29	73.7
1-3/4	4.4	30	76.2
2	5.1	31	78.7
2-1/2	6.4	32	81.3
3	7.6	33	83.8
3-1/2	8.9	34	86.4
4	10.2	35	88.9
4-1/2	11.4	36	91.4
5	12.7	37	94.0
6	15.2	38	96.5
7	17.8	39	99.1
8	20.3	40	101.6
9	22.9	41	104.1
10	25.4	42	106.7
11	27.9	43	109.2
12	30.5	44	111.8
13	33.0	45	114.3
14	35.6	46	116.8
15	38.1	47	119.4
16	40.6	48	121.9
17	43.2	49	124.5
18	45.7	50	127.0
19	48.3		

Volumes

1 fluid ounce	29.6 ml
1 pint	.473 l
1 quart	.946 l
1 gallon	3.785 l

Weights

0.035 oz.	1 gram
1 oz.	28.4 gram
1 lb.	453.6 grams

Temperatures

To convert Celsius to Fahrenheit, multiply by 9, divide by 5, and add 32. To convert Fahrenheit to Celsius, subtract 32, multiply by 5, and divide by 9.

Acknowledgements

— 🌿 —

My special thanks go to

My "children," Laura Ling, Dr. David Ling, David Carroll, and Patrick Carroll, for their love, friendship, help, encouragement, and acceptance; and to my precious darling girl, granddaughter Leah Caroline Ling.

Evan Bracken, photographer (Light Reflections, Hendersonville, NC), wizard with a camera and kindred spirit bearing recipes.

Chris Rich, my Altamont Press editor, whose patience and expertise made this project fun.

Pauline "Precious" Roberson, friend of long standing who sews, grows, and helps with shows.

Allen Stanford, friend, gardener, travel-to-shows companion, and Jack-of-all-trades helper.

Elaine Thompson, art director at Altamont Press, whose talent is evident throughout this book.

Thanks also to

Kerry Clark (River Valley Inn, P.O. Box 594, Valle Crucis, NC), for allowing us to photograph my work (page 104) in her charming bed-and-breakfast inn.

Dawn Cusick, Altamont Press editor, for help with photography and for walking my outline into the publishing house.

Jeanette and William Edmiston, "neighbors" at the farmers' market whose humor and friendship are precious to me.

Virgil Horney III (Horney's Hollow, High Point, NC) for help growing scented geraniums and lavender varieties.

Linda Brooks Jones (Grey Gables Inn, P.O. Box 5252, Rugby, TN), a wonderful hostess, marvelous cook, poet, and new friend.

Cindra at Meadows Direct (R.R. Box 75, Onslaw, Iowa 52321) for freeze-drying specific colors of roses for any custom work.

Jeanne and Chuck Morton for permitting us to photograph scenes at their Black Mountain Herbfest (Bee Tree Farms, P.O. Box 1251, Black Mountain, NC).

Carolyn Owen, landscape gardener from Summerfield, NC, for her assistance in designing my Sara gardens.

Beth Payne (Onion Knob Herbs, Rte. 4, Box 238, Taylorsville, NC), for help with weddings, wildcrafting, and growing.

Julia Pedigo (faculty member, Appalachian State University), for permitting us to photograph the custom window treatments (page 50) I made for her.

Donna Eberle Redmond, for help getting me started on my new path.

Dianne Reichard, generous friend who made me chocolates and helped with Latin names.

Cindy Sash, whose companionship, time, energy, and enthusiasm eased my gardening season after Louie died.

Jill Mark Sasser, Carolyn Wolfe, and Jane Karrh, for helping hostess tours.

Carol Taylor, Altamont Press editor who first "discovered" me at a craft show.

Peggy Watts (Rivershore Herbs, Elizabeth City, NC), kindred spirit who starts my herb plants and delivers them to me in late May for planting in my gardens.

Roy Weaver for sharing information, plants, and cuttings of herbs and wildflowers, and for allowing me to harvest pussy willows along the creek banks of his "Eden."

Carolyn Wolfe (Fleetwood, NC), for allowing us to photograph my work (page 115) in her lovely mountain home.

The staff at Broyhill Chapel (Mars Hill University, NC) for allowing us to photograph the herbal wedding.

The Herbal Green Pages

—An Herbal Resource Guide—

Maureen Rogers, Editor

The Herb Growing and Marketing Network
P.O. Box 245
Silver Springs, PA 17575

Index